technical
charting
for
profits

Randall
chart your future

Mark Larson
$

Wiley Online Trading for a Living

technical charting for profits

MARK L. LARSON

JOHN WILEY & SONS, INC.
New York • Chichester • Weinheim • Brisbane • Singapore • Toronto

Published by John Wiley & Sons, Inc.
Published simultaneously in Canada.

This publication is designed to provide accurate and authoritative information in regard to the subject matter covered. It is sold with the understanding that the publisher is not engaged in rendering professional services. If professional advice or other expert assistance is required, the services of a competent professional person should be sought.

Designations used by companies to distinguish their products are often claimed as trademarks. In all instances where John Wiley & Sons, Inc., is aware of a claim, the product names appear in initial capital or all capital letters. Readers, however, should contact the appropriate companies for more complete information regarding trademarks and registration.

TeleChart 2000, TC2000, and StockFinder are registered trademarks of Worden Brothers, Inc.
Balance of Power, MoneyStream, and Time Segmented Volume are trademarks of Worden Brothers, Inc.
LEAPS is a registered trademark of the Options Exchange.
Software services for Figure 5.4 provided by All-Tech Direct, Inc.

Library of Congress Cataloging-in-Publication Data:
Larson, Mark L., 1965-
    Technical charting for profits / Mark L. Larson.
       p.   cm.—(Wiley online trading for a living)
    Includes index.
    ISBN 0-471-41324-0 (cloth : alk. paper)
      1. Electronic trading on securities.   2. Day trading (Securities)
   3. Stocks—Prices—Computer network resources.   4. Investments—Computer network resources. I. Title. II. Series.
    HF4515 .95 .L37 2001
    332.63'2042—dc21   00-064921

Printed in the United States of America.

10 9 8 7 6 5 4 3 2 1

preface

As times change so does technology, and with the change of technology comes more opportunity. Opportunity is simply defined as one's ability to react. And when investing in the stock market, it's those who react who become successful investors; those who don't react are the unsuccessful investors. Technology's greatest change can be seen with investors who now see the need to know what investments to select and when is the ideal entry and exit point. Earlier generations used the simpler method of investing by allowing someone else to make all of their financial decisions for them. But then came the baby boomers (both male and female investors). They have elected to take on more responsibility for their own investments, and so have made a commitment to acquire more knowledge for a better understanding of what we call Wall Street.

This book, unlike many other financial books, emphasizes hands-on knowledge with "simplicity." First I provide a history of the stock market, then explain step by step how the stock market has changed and why these changes offer investors more opportunity. The largest portion of the book focuses on the technical analysis of the stock market and the tools that are needed to make a more educated investment decision.

Times have changed in the investment world; today it's not just the fundamentals of a company that are important. As the stock market continues to grow, so does its volatility. Because of volatility, now more than ever it's important to understand and implement technical analysis indicators. Understanding technical analysis can be as difficult as trying to understand a foreign language. This book explains in laymen's terms such technical terms as "Support and Resistance Levels," "MoneyStream," "Time Segmented Volume," "Moving Averages," and other indicators, utilizing charts as examples. Now you too can understand the value of these indicators and be able to implement them into your financial toolbox.

After you complete the chapters on technical analysis, I'll take you through the understanding of option investing and its power. Chapters 11, 12, 13 will cover monthly income strategies and priceless information on how to reduce your tax liability while protecting your assets from everyone.

MARK L. LARSON

San Francisco, CA
December 2000

acknowledgments

I wish to extend a special word of thanks to Worden Brothers, Inc., of Durham, North Carolina. Their existence has helped open the doors of financial opportunity, providing investors with an understanding of when to buy and, more important, when to sell an investment. As a member of their service for many years, I appreciate their hard work and dedication as industry leaders, staying ahead of the changes in a fast-moving business. My hat goes off to all of you—Peter, Chris, Don, Patrick, and Craig. Next I'd like to thank Eric S. Hadik of www.insiidetrac.com for his monthly reports, which give me an outlook on what can affect the stock market and how; the people at All-Tech Direct, www.attain.com, and RealTick for the technology of direct execution; and, finally, my colleagues at www.incometrader.com, www.writingputs.com, and www.mytradecentral.com.

A large amount of time goes into writing a book, and once again I want to thank you, the readers of my first book, *Trade Stocks Online*, for your support and requests for a clearly written technical book that could be easily understood. Because of you I continue to push the envelope of knowledge, striving not to be the wealthiest in assets but the wealthiest in knowledge. Knowledge isn't rated by what you know; it's rated by how you apply that knowledge. May each of you continue to acquire more knowledge and understanding of technical analysis and the benefits they offer. These tools add an additional value to the future of your investments.

Special loving thanks go out to all of my family members for their support and understanding. Because of my passion for what I do, I live, breathe, and sleep (sometimes) for educating others. And because they recognize my passion, they understand and support me when I lock myself in my office staring at technical indicators as I type away. And as for my nieces and nephews, thank you for teaching me how to play freeze tag. It's because of children that I continue to focus on the future of the financial monster "money." May our government wake up some day and teach people the value of money and how to properly plan for a more rewarding future and retirement. I hope it will open up the school systems and allow the knowledge of finance to be taught to young children so they don't grow up wondering what retirement is before it's too late to plan.

Finally, I'd like to publicly thank the kind, hardworking people at John Wiley & Sons for publishing my works; and Amazon.com, Barnes & Noble Booksellers, and Borders book stores for inviting me to visit them and their readers throughout the country as we all work together towards planning a successful future.

M.L.L.

contents

chapter 1

planning your profits

As I begin this, my second book, I ask myself: "What motivates me to write a second book?" Is it the mere knowledge that I can do it; is it the relief of transforming what's in my mind to paper; or is it the thought that a good book can help other investors? In all sincerity, all of these things help me to write, but the key motivator is the ability to help others have a better understanding of this foreign language we know as the stock market. While money is an important factor of life, our educational system doesn't teach us how to invest or plan for our retirement.

Think about your days in school; most people don't even take a basic class of finance that teaches the dos and don'ts of investing. Most people can't even properly balance a checkbook. Even worse, our own government can't figure out how to reduce our country's budget. Perhaps the problem with our government is the fact that when it needs more money, it just prints more. Not so for those of us who run low on money. We as individuals have only two choices: Get a job and/or be sure our money is working for us. I prefer the second method and would much rather allow my money to work for me. There's something to be said about knowing your money is working for you regardless of what you're doing. The most important fact about money is *knowledge*.

As times have changed and over 75 million baby boomers plan

for their retirement days, we no longer can rely on living off of Social Security. The future of your retirement will come from the money that is working for you, which enables you to make decisions that control your money. Your financial knowledge truly will determine how you and your family will care for each other during your working years and your retirement years. I can recall my parents and grandparents always saying to get ahead in life, I needed to study hard at school, go to college, and then find a good-paying job. Sorry, things aren't that easy. I came from a family that had less than no money; at times we could barely afford school clothes. Is this the fault of my parents or of our society?

I would have to say our society because the lack of financial schooling forces investors to pay others to make financial decisions for them. However, you determine why you rely on others to manage your finances. It's a lack of knowledge that forces investors to rely on others to make their decisions. Today more investors realize that it's time to take more control of their own financial destiny. It is not just the baby boomers who have led this change; the computer and technology have enabled investors more opportunity to do their own research and place their own trades.

The history of the stock market has shown great growth and opportunity with very little signs of stopping. However, with the change of our population and demand for individual wealth, the stock market is experiencing something known as volatility. Simply explained, volatility is nothing more than a lot of buying and selling within short time frames. Investors of past decades purchased stocks to hold onto long term, regardless of the outcome. In today's volatile environment, the old school theory of buying and holding forever has changed; more profits are being taken in a shorter time frame. As we witness the changes in the stock market, brokerage firms are forced to make the changes investors want to see. Some of the changes that have already occurred are the reduction of commissions, the ability to execute trades online, real-time stock and option quotes, and, most important, technical analysis charting.

By utilizing charting patterns and indicators, investors dramatically increase their ability to select the proper time to buy and sell stocks. Investors have learned to examine the stock market regularly, as doctors would examine a patient. Doctors rely on their educated knowledge and such tools as an X ray. Investors are now relying on their educated knowledge and technical charts. Even with all the tools we have today, Americans are still brainwashed into thinking that they should buy and hold long term to avoid paying taxes now. I'm sorry; I'd rather be taxed today, knowing what my tax liabilities are now, instead of hoping they will be lower when I'm retired.

When investors have the proper knowledge, they will realize the advantages of taking profits sooner rather than later. This subject is explained in Chapter 13 as knowledgeable investors treat their investments as a business and operate as a corporation. Investors have to understand that the key to investing is to know when to take some profits and then decide when to reenter a trade again. Don't get me wrong. I don't mind having long-term investments—we all need them. But as a business investor, I also like to cash out with reasonable profits and diversify into other investments. The stock market will not always continue to be bullish and go up. As I look at my real-time quote system (provided by www.alltech.com), I feel the pain for the thousands and thousands of investors who are put out of business when we experience a bearish correction in the Dow or Nasdaq Composite.

It's sad to say but all good things must come to an end. Any investor can make money in a bullish upward market, but 90 percent of investors don't know how to invest in a bearish downward market. Can you identify the beginning of a bearish market trend? Volatility and profit taking also affect the stock market even as unemployment decreases to all-time lows. However, a large group of investors who thought that making money was as easy as pushing a button (to buy or sell a stock online) or calling their broker lose money because of large corrections that occur. As an investor you always have to wonder what is in store for the stock market. As we approached the new millennium, many investors went back to cash to be safe, yet the largest majority of investors added money, as the stock market ended the year setting new historical highs in both the Dow and Nasdaq. And shortly after the new millennium our economy began to look strong as more and more money went back into the stock market. Another bullish run seemed to be beginning.

Then came April 2000 when the bull decided to quit running and appeared to give in to the bear as we began a true stock market correction, one that many investors never experienced before.

This wasn't just a short-term monthly correction, it truly was a bearish correction that would stay with us for many months. This bearish correction created big problems for thousands and thousands of investors who didn't have the right mind-set and knowledge of what to do or how to react. What does the term "correction" really mean? To me it's any time a stock can be bought at a much lower price than its strongest Support Level or when the stock drops below its 200-day Moving Average. As for the Dow and Nasdaq Composite, a true correction occurs when they each break below their strongest Support Levels and begin testing their 200-day Moving Average. Bearish corrections below strong Support Levels and 200-day Moving Averages are not immediate signs to buy. Determining when to actually buy should only be done after viewing other technicals to assure

figure 1.1 Dow Jones Industrials (DJ-30)

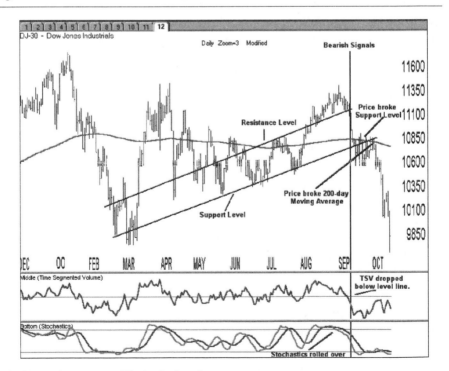

TC2000.com chart courtesy of Worden Brothers, Inc.

figure 1.2   Nasdaq Composite Index (COMPQX)

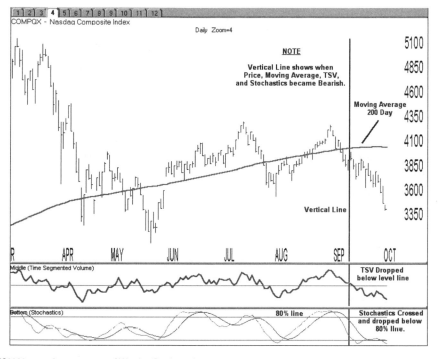

TC2000.com chart courtesy of Worden Brothers, Inc.

yourself the stock has stopped dropping in value. (See Figures 1.1 and 1.2.)

The greatest way to be part of a bearish market is to know how to short the market (make money as an individual stock or the indexes drop in value) or not be invested at all. However, with the recent rewards of the past market history, as more and more money continued to flood the market, investors were not slowing down. And as more and more money entered the stock market, more and more companies found an opportunity to take their companies public as IPOs (initial public offerings). Investors should have learned a very valuable lesson about the stock market. The only positive side of the bearish correction will be that more investors will acquire more hands-on experience and know when to take some profits off the table and diversify some of their investments into real estate, for example. Or better yet, they should pay off their debt or reduce their largest debt, their house mortgage. (Remember, your house mortgage is not only your largest asset but for many people it's also their largest debt.) There isn't a person in the stock market who couldn't say "I should have taken some profits," but instead people just continue to increase their lifestyle instead of properly planning for their retirement. Of course, taking profits is easier said than done as brokerage firms are still encouraging investors to add more money to their portfolio instead of taking more profits out of their accounts.

The same goes for the saying "Buy good stocks on margin and hold long term." It's a great idea, but again, how long should investors hold onto a stock? Until they retire, or until they can take a guaranteed profit and move on to another investment risking only their original capital? I choose to take profits when I see fit. Use the business practice of "cash to asset, back to cash."

Today's investors need to understand that true losses are measured not only in dollar amounts but also in the lost opportunity that the money will not be able to produce. As we have seen in past corrections, investors lose money and at the same time the stock market loses investors. Within some brokerage firms, more than one-third of investor accounts were closed during the April 2000 correction. The closure of these accounts left the investors with a complete financial loss. I believe that those numbers were on the conservative side, because the correction also made potential investors think twice about entering the market. Many people continue to stand on the sidelines. The old saying goes, all things must come to an end, and for some investors it was an ugly ending to a bearish stock market correction as the bull rolled over and the bear market began. Again the largest problem with a bear market is that 90 percent or more of the investors don't know how to invest in a downward market, which can leave them with a complete financial loss during times like that. I'm repeating this to you investors so that next time the stock market shows indications of a bearish correction, you'll reconsider the bullish outlook of your investments. Prepare for the corrections and get the proper knowledge so you're able to react sooner rather than later.

The first lesson begins with discipline and the ability of technically knowing which direction an individual stock or market may move. I've made it a professional point of discipline not to guess or predict what the stock market will do each day but only to react accordingly by trading long or short strategies. If the market is bullish, I consider bullish investments; when the market is bearish, I consider bearish investments. The key to investing is knowing how to make money in all market directions and conditions. However, when the market shows continuous signs of corrections and volatility, many investors stand on the sidelines rather than profiting from both opportunities.

The two most common investment opportunities for a bearish market are known as shorting stock and buying put options on either individual stocks or stock indexes. These techniques are not new to the industry, but many investors miss these opportunities because they lack knowledge. I don't understand why investors don't invest in bearish corrections and why brokerage firms are not educating investors how to hedge their portfolio with these bearish strategies. When was the last time your broker called you and advised you to take some profits and stand on the sideline for a while? Figure 1.3 shows Microsoft at its highs and then several months later at its lows. As a technical trader I would have exited MSFT during its highs, surely if it broke below its Support Level of $100. The only calls I received from brokers were when they wanted me to invest more money long term. Think about it: How often does your broker advise you to take some profits and pay off your debt or mortgage? There is always more opportunity to buy again. If you've received this kind of call from your broker, then that broker is unique, paying attention to your profits and not his or her own.

Now don't get me wrong; I'm not bashing brokers. I just want you to understand that your account should be invested just as a brokerage firm invests its own money. This means that you should *always* be prepared to take profits when they occur and even more, to change your investment objectives according to market conditions. You must understand how and when to make money in a downward market. How important is it to invest in a downward market? It's just as important as investing in an upward bullish market. Cash is cash. Regardless of whether it's earned in a bullish or a bearish market, it still rewards your future with the same opportunities. The most astonishing part of the stock market is how it continues to

figure 1.3   Microsoft Corp. (MSFT)

TC2000.com chart courtesy of Worden Brothers, Inc.

change over time. I never dreamed that today I would be able to buy and sell stocks on the Internet. And more important, I never thought that a chart could be used to indicate when and what stocks to buy and sell.

Looking back on the history of the stock market, we can see that there have been many great changes. The most important technological change has allowed individual investors the capability of viewing a stock's past, present, and future performance, which provides them with a better understanding of a stock's direction. In the past investors would buy a stock based on advice and not view a chart of the stock's past performance, which in reality is a very risky way to make an investment. Yet today we can view a chart, which shows us such indicators as Stochastics, MoneyStream, Balance of Power, MACDs, Moving Averages, and Time Segmented Volume, among others. Investors who use good charting services are wiser investors who are rewarded with profits. More important, they're able to limit their losses. Greater profits and limited losses are what bring me to writing this book as I will explain in simple terms how to use the technical charting service provided by TC2000.com.

Before we cover the many different technical indicators used in today's stock market, I'm going to take you back in time and give you a better understanding of the stock market and, I hope, an even better understanding of how times have changed and will continue to change in the future. Change is good—but only if you know how to react to it.

Chapter 1 Quiz

1. The largest contribution to the strong "bullish" stock market can be attributed to the investment of which group:

    a. stock brokers   b. corporate investments   c. baby boomers

2. In April 2000, a bearish sell-off affected over 30 percent of investors because of which of the following?

    a. investors took profits   b. margin calls

3. Today's investors are more concerned about which one of the following?

    a. tax obligations   b. knowledge   c. retirement

4. By using technical analysis indicators, an investor can review the past, present, and limited future information.

    a. true   b. false

5. Bearish corrections are commonly recognized when an investment drops below which of the three Moving Averages?

    a. 50 day   b. 100 day   c. 200 day

6. The stock market has changed over time. Investors of the past relied on information about a company's fundamentals only, yet today many investors find that technical analysis is just as important if not more so.

    a. true   b. false

7. Which two of the following are technical indicators?

    a. stochastics   b. moving bands   c. time segmented volume

8. The term "IPO" means initial public offering, which is when a company first offers its company stock to public investors.

    a. true   b. false

9. When investors are looking to profit from a bearish market condition, they may elect to invest by utilizing which two of these strategies?

    a. buy put options   b. sell naked puts   c. go short

10. What creates a lot of volatility within the stock market?

    a. excessive buying   b. excessive selling   c. both

Chapter 1 Quiz Answers

1. The largest percentage growth of the stock market can be attributed to the *baby boomers*, who have a better understanding of how to plan for their retirement.

2. A large percentage of the April 2000 market crash was due to *margin calls*. A margin call is a point at which an investor's account balance has dropped below the brokerage firm's minimum requirement. Most firms allow investors to borrow as much as 50 percent of their total investment amount. When we experience a correction such as the one in April 2000, investors have minimum amount of time to get funds into their accounts. This time frame ranges from 24 to 72 hours.

3. As strange as it may be, investors are still more concerned about their *tax obligations* when selling early than they are with acquiring the proper knowledge.

4. *True*. Because of technology, investors have the capability of making more educated investment decisions by analyzing a stock's history. Investors do this when utilizing charting services (technical indicators which show a stock/index's price movement), which allow them to see how a stock has performed in the past, how it's performing currently, and, most important, how may it perform in the future.

5. Of the three different Moving Averages—50, 100, and 200 day—it's the *200-day Moving Average* that has the biggest weight on the next direction of the stock/index. Many people believe that when a stock breaks below its longest-term average of 200, the stock/index is in a bearish correction. This was experienced in April 2000. The shorter Moving Averages are more relevant to investors who elect not to hold long term.

6. *True*. Technical indicators have given investors a better understanding and edge on when it's best to enter and exit a trade. Fundamentals enable investors to view how a company has done from a financial point of view; however, it's

the technical indicators that provide investors a better understanding of when and how a stock may react in different market conditions.

7. *Stochastics* and *Time Segmented Volume* are technical indicators. Stochastics are helpful indicators that enable an investor to find better entry and exit points based on when a stock is overbought or oversold. Time Segmented Volume is used as an indicator that charts a stock's pattern based on both the price and volume movement of the stock.

8. *True.* An IPO is an initial public offering of a company's stock. It is a form of raising money by allowing investors to buy a portion of the company.

9. The two common ways investors can profit in a downward market is to *buy put options* on selected stocks or indexes or to *go short* on the stock or index, the more common choice of brokerage firms.

10. Both *excessive buying* and *excessive selling* create volatility. As the stock market continues to grow and as more investors utilize the market as an alternative source of investment, more investors are buying and selling. Times have changed; investors don't buy only to hold long term. Many investors elect to take profits when an investment increases by 20 percent or more.

chapter 2

Wall Street as it began

How did Wall Street begin? Wall Street takes its name from a wall of brush and mud that was built alongside the street's original pathway. The Dutch settlers built the wall shortly after establishing a trading post on the island of Manhattan in 1609. In 1626 the Dutch purchased the entire island from the local Indians with trinkets and beads worth the equivalent of $24. After they purchased the island, the Dutch improved the wall to keep their cows in and the Indians out. The path known as Wall Street quickly became the center for commercial and community activity that connected the docks serving the Hudson River on the west and the East River docks. The connection between the west and east rivers allowed for importing of goods between the different merchants who then built their homes and businesses close by. And of course, soon after homes and businesses were built, a city hall and church were erected. Although stocks and bonds were not known at this time, merchants bought and sold such commodities as tobacco, furs, and molasses.

In 1664 the English gained control of the area and the settlement was renamed New York. Between 1785 and 1790, New York City was the capital of the United States. In 1789 George Washington was inaugurated president on the steps of the Federal Hall on Wall Street, and a few months later the first U.S. Congress met in the same building. Stocks and bonds were still unheard of.

The first order of financial trade was to authorize the issuance of $80 million in government bonds to help pay for the war against England. These bonds became the first national securities available for trading. Two years later, when bank stocks were added, the world of financial investing was about to begin.

On May 17, 1792, 24 brokers met under a buttonwood tree at what is now 68 Wall Street, forming the first organized stock market in New York. Their agreement, known as the Buttonwood Agreement, was the beginning of what is now known as New York Stock Exchange. It allowed these 24 brokers to trade with one another beneath that buttonwood tree. In 1817 the exchange was moved from beneath the buttonwood tree to a rented room at 40 Wall Street. The first corporate stock traded under the Buttonwood Agreement was the Bank of New York.

On March 8, 1817, the constitution of rules for conduct of business was adopted. The organization was named New York Stock & Exchange Board. However, on January 29, 1863, the name was shortened and changed to New York Stock Exchange, a name that has continued to this day.

On November 15, 1867, a decision was made to simplify the way investors would be able to identify investment companies. Ticker symbols were developed, which we still use today to identify investment companies. General Electric, for example, is commonly known on Wall Street by its ticker symbol GE. Stocks can be identified as to which exchange they trade on—New York or Nasdaq—by the number of letters in each ticker symbol. Stocks traded on the New York Exchange use one, two, or three letters as a ticker symbol. Stocks traded on the Nasdaq Exchange have four- or five-letter ticker symbols. This fact is of great importance when buying or selling stocks because the ticker symbol identifies whether the stock is offered by a market maker (Nasdaq) or specialist on the major exchange (NYSE). Stocks are like retail products and are stored until needed. At that time they are taken from the inventory warehouse and sold to the investors. New York Stock Exchange stocks are offered by what are known as specialists; Nasdaq stocks are offered by market makers. The New York Exchange has one specialist for each stock. Nasdaq stocks are offered by many market makers, who offer different prices for different Nasdaq stocks. Both New York and Nasdaq stocks are traded on different exchanges, such as the Chicago, American, Pacific, and Philadelphia exchanges.

As the interest in the New York exchange grew, so did the demand for more brokers. To become a member of the New York Exchange, a broker had to purchase a seat. That's right, a seat, and it wasn't a very comfortable one. In the early days it was a hard wooden chair. By purchasing a chair, a broker gained the right to be a part of the exchange and to sit in that chair marketing his inventory (company stocks) to other investors. The lowest price paid for a seat (also known as a membership) was $4,000 in 1876 and 1878. If you think inflation has been climbing as well as the stock market, so has the value of the exchange membership seats. The last two seats recently sold at record high prices: $2,600,000 on March 1, 1999, and $2,650,000 on August 23, 1999.

Brokers who were unable to afford a seat on the exchange or who were refused a membership often found it very difficult to make a living by trading securities. During poor market conditions they went broke. Don't forget: Once brokers purchase a seat, they must also have the financial backing to warehouse their stocks (buy and sell the inventory).

So how do market makers/specialists make money? The answer is: simply by purchasing stocks at the bid price (the lower price) and turning around and selling the stock at the ask price (the higher price). The difference of the two prices is known as "in the spread."

Example: XYZ stock is offered at $39^1/_4 \times 39^1/_2$, and as investors we buy the stock at the ask price, here $39^1/_2$. Now, if we were to sell XYZ stock, we would be selling it at the bid price of $39^1/_4$. Simple math shows us that the difference between the bid and ask price is one-quarter of a percent. In essence, every time there's a buyer, there's also a seller. It is the responsibility of the specialist or market maker to execute the trade. At times the spread (price between the bid and ask) changes. Some days the spread is lower and other days the spread is higher. Spread changes when a stock has more volatility—investors decide to buy or sell at the same time as a large majority of other investors. Good news increases the spread between the bid and ask price as more buyers purchase. The opposite occurs with bad news; the spread between the bid and the ask is reduced as more sellers sell.

Don't be enticed if you see a lower spread than usual. The reason for that spread is not to benefit you, the investor. Lower spreads between bid and ask prices show that there is a lack of interest in the stock at that moment; higher spreads can indicate a greater interest in the stock at that time. The key point to remember is that market makers/specialists always price the stock according to whether there are more buyers or more sellers. More buyers lead to a higher ask price; more sellers lead to a lower bid price.

When buying or selling equities, it is always safer to use a limit order, which is a set price. Investors who elect to buy or sell securities at the market price are willing to allow the trade to occur at the current price, which can change in just a matter of seconds. Using limit orders ensures that the trade will occur only at a selected price or the order is not executed.

As the years have passed, the stock market hours have changed. On December 1, 1873, New York implemented trading hours of 10 A.M. to 3 P.M. Monday through Friday and 10 A.M. to noon on Saturdays, Eastern Standard Time. Today's stock market hours are currently Monday through Friday 9:30 A.M. to 4:00 P.M. Eastern Standard Time. Periodically the stock market considers extending weekly hours and enabling investors more opportunity to trade the market later into the afternoon; someday we again may see Saturday trading. Will this be an advantage to investors? I don't believe extended hours will do much more than reduce market volatility and limit the effect market makers and specialists have on a stock's price. Breaking news today enables them to raise or lower a stock's price.

The changes of the past have paved the roads of the future for both the Dow Jones Industrial Average and Nasdaq Composite. Such changes as trading hours, execution systems, and technical indicators have opened more doors for investors.

timeline—history of NYSE

October 23, 1868
Memberships are made salable; prior to this time each member had a reserved seat in a particular place and had a right to the seat for life.

February 1, 1869
The New York Stock Exchange (NYSE) requires registering of securities by listed companies to prevent their overissuance.

May 8, 1869
The NYSE and Open Board of Brokers adopts a plan of consolidation.

September 24, 1869
Gold speculation results in "Black Friday." A large group of financiers tries to corner the gold market and precipitates a business panic followed by a depression.

November 13, 1878
The first telephones are installed on the trading floor.

December 15, 1886
First million-share day; 1,200,000 shares are traded.

January 23, 1895
The NYSE recommends that listed companies publish and distribute to stockholders annual financial statements.

April 23, 1903
The NYSE occupies a new building with current trading floor at 18 Broad Street.

July 31, 1914
The NYSE is closed through December 11 due to World War I in Europe.

October 13, 1915
The base of quoting and trading in stocks changes from percent of par value to dollars.

April 26, 1920
The Stock Clearing Corporation is established to facilitate the validation, delivery, and settlement of securities.

October 29, 1929
The Dow drops 17 percent in October, marking the start of a period of high unemployment rates and economic stagnation known as the Great Depression.

March 4, 1933
The NYSE is closed until March 14 for bank holiday.

May 27, 1933
The Securities Act of 1933 is enacted. Its two basic purposes: to provide full disclosure to investors and to prohibit fraud in connection with the sale of securities.

June 6, 1934
The Securities Act of 1934 is enacted, providing for the regulation of securities trading and the establishment of Securities and Exchange Commission (SEC).

July 14, 1966
A new NYSE Composite Index is inaugurated.

December 20, 1966
Transmission of trade and quote data from the exchange floor is fully automated.

December 28, 1967
Muriel Siebert becomes the first female member of the NYSE.

February 12, 1970
Joseph L. Searles III becomes the first black member of the NYSE.

March 26, 1970
Public ownership of NYSE membership is approved.

April 9, 1970
Donaldson, Lufkin & Jenrette becomes the first member firm to go public.

October 28, 1970
Alice Jarcho is the first woman member of the NYSE to regularly work on the trading floor.

February 18, 1971
The New York Stock Exchange is incorporated.

July 27, 1971
The first member organization is listed—Merrill Lynch.

May 11, 1973
The Depository Trust Company is established to provide a central depository for securities certificates and electronically record transfers of stock ownership.

October 1, 1974
The NYSE extends its trading hours to 4 P.M. Eastern Standard Time.

April 30, 1975
The fixed commission system is abolished, enabling brokerage firms to charge customers as they please.

January 19, 1976
A new high-speed data line begins transmitting market data at up to 36,000 characters a minute.

March 4, 1976
Alternative listing standards are adopted to facilitate listings of major foreign corporations.

May 24, 1976
Specialists begin holding odd lots in their stock.

February 3, 1977
Foreign broker/dealers are permitted to obtain memberships in the NYSE.

August 18, 1982
First 100-million-share day: 132,681,120 shares are traded.

November 6, 1984
The NYSE is open on presidential Election Day for the first time ever.

March 28, 1985
Ronald Reagan becomes the first U.S. President to visit the NYSE while in office.

September 30, 1985
Trading hours are changed to 9:30 A.M.–4 P.M. Eastern Standard Time.

November 7, 1988
The NYSE opens an office in London to help European companies gain access to the U.S. capital markets and the listings on the exchange.

June 13, 1991
The NYSE begins its first off-hours trading sessions. Two crossing sessions extend trading activity to 5:15 P.M.

May 17, 1992
The NYSE celebrates its 200th anniversary with a series of commemorative events.

May 22, 1995
The trading posts upgrade is completed as part of the ongoing Integrated Technology Plan.

June 1, 1995
Richard A. Grasso is elected chairman and chief executive officer of NYSE, the first to be promoted to that position from the professional staff.

June 7, 1995
Securities settlement is shortened from five to three days following the trade date. Today this is known as trading day plus three days (T+3).

November 15, 1996
Vimpel-Communications becomes the first Russian-listed company to be traded on the NYSE.

June 24, 1997
The NYSE begins trading stocks in sixteenths, an interim step toward quoting stock prices in decimals.

October 27, 1997
The largest-ever drop in the Dow Jones Industrial Average occurs—554 points in one trading day. The circuit breaker rule goes into effect for the first time, halting trading at 3:30 P.M.

October 28, 1997
First billion-share day: 1,202,550,000 shares are traded. The Dow Jones Industrial Average soars 337.17 points, closing at its biggest single-day gain.

April 15, 1998
The new circuit breaker rule goes into effect to halt trading when the Dow Jones Industrial Average drops 10 percent, 20 percent, and 30 percent.

October 26, 1998
DaimlerChrysler becomes the first international corporation to list its ordinary shares on the NYSE.

December 22, 1998
The NYSE reaches a new preliminary agreement to build a new trading facility on the block across from the current exchange building. Growth of the NYSE continues.

April 13, 2000
The Dow Jones Industrial Average and Nasdaq both close down over 500 points. Signs of true bear market correct as over one-third of investors are taken out of the market due to margin calls.

I hope you have found this chapter to be as interesting to read as I did to write. Although there are millions of investors worldwide, only a small number know the great history of Wall Street.

Chapter 2 Quiz

1. The name "Wall Street" comes from a wall that was built of which two materials in 1609?

   a. stones   b. brush   c. mud

2. What was the first financial order of trade at the New York Stock Exchange?

   a. railroad stocks   b. coal   c. government bonds

3. What year did the New York Stock Exchange agree to simplify the way investors identify companies that traded on it?

   a. 1863   b. 1867   c. 1869

4. On August 23, 19__, a new price record was set as a seat on the New York Stock Exchange sold for $2,650,000.

   a. 95   b. 97   c. 99

5. In what year were the first telephones allowed to be used on the New York Stock Exchange?

   a. 1868   b. 1873   c. 1878

6. From July 11 until December 14, 1914, the New York Stock Exchange was closed because of World War I.

   a. true   b. false

7. To this day brokerage firms are still regulated by the Securities and Exchange Commission and must follow SEC guidelines.

   a. true   b. false

8. Which president was the first to visit the New York Stock Exchange while in office?

   a. President Gerald Ford   b. President Ronald Reagan

   c. President George Bush

9. On October 28, 1997, the New York Stock Exchange traded over 1 billion shares in a single trading session.

   a. true   b. false

10. On April 13, 2000, both the New York Stock Exchange and the Nasdaq Composite each suffered their worse single day loss as both indexes closed down over how many points?

    a. 400 points   b. 500 points   c. 600 points

Chapter 2 Quiz Answers

1. During 1609 the Dutch settlers build a wall of *brush* and *mud* after establishing a trading post on the island of Manhattan.

2. The first order of trade on the New York Stock Exchange was *government bonds*, which were used to fund the English War.

3. On November 15, *1867*, the NYSE simplified the way publicly traded company names were to be identified by implementing what is still today known as ticker symbols. Example: General Electric is identified by its ticker symbol "GE."

4. In *1999*, the most expensive seat on the New York Stock Exchange sold for $2,650,000. The first seat sold for $4,000.

5. During the year *1878*, telephones were allowed at the New York Stock Exchange for the first time ever.

6. *True*. The New York Stock Exchange closed from July 11 until December 14, 1914, in memory of those serving in World War I in England.

7. *False*. As of April 30, 1975, regulated commissions were abolished. Now brokerage firms can charge as they please.

8. On March 3, 1985, *President Ronald Reagan* was the first sitting president to visit the New York Stock Exchange.

9. *True*. October 28, 1997, was the first day the NYSE traded over 1 billion shares in a single day; its total was 1,202,500,000. This also was the biggest single-point gain for the NYSE; it closed up 337.17 points. Both single-day records have been beaten since that time.

10. On April 13, 2000, both the New York Stock Exchange and the Nasdaq Composite closed down over *500* points each, setting a record for the first time both exchanges closed down over *500* points in one trading session. That day was the beginning of the first bear market correction in decades.

chapter 3

Support and Resistance Levels

It is easy to define Support and Resistance Levels by viewing chart patterns of stocks or indexes. These and many other patterns have become very valuable when determining when to buy and sell investments. Support and Resistance Levels are simple indicators that can indicate a change of direction in a stock or index. Support and Resistance Levels are also known in Wall Street as supply and demand. And we all know that it's supply and demand that move the market up and down. Support and Resistance Levels are simply a point at which investors elect to buy and sell an investment. Although these levels can be seen visually (as in the examples given in this chapter), they are initiated by the mental mind-set of investors. For example, let's assume that XYZ stock is trading at $75. After we make the purchase, it then trades down below $75 to $67. A person's natural reaction is to consider selling the stock when it increases back to $75. That's what happens as many investors do the same with stocks that trade within what is known as a trading range or trend. They identify the point at which a stock tests its higher-price range "resistance" and then drops down to its "support" lower level.

Support Levels

A Support Level is just what it sounds like: a point when a stock's price is supported at a certain value as an increase in volume accumulates and begins to show signs of an upward bullish movement. The longer a Support Level can be held, the larger the opportunity may be for an upward bullish movement. Support Levels are used very often with individual stocks and with indexes, such as the Dow Jones Industrial Average and the Nasdaq Composite. It's important to understand that Support Levels are not just patterns that are shown from a left-to-right horizontal direction, as in Figure 3.1. These levels are also common during upward or downward movements of an individual stock or index. Figure 3.2 shows a strong upward Support Level during a rising bullish trend. Figure 3.3 shows a Support Level during a bearish downward trend.

To project the future Support Level of a stock's trading pattern, one might choose to use trend lines. They can be drawn on your computer screen by clicking the mouse on "Tools" (upper left corner),

figure 3.1   Nokia Corp. Ads (NOK)

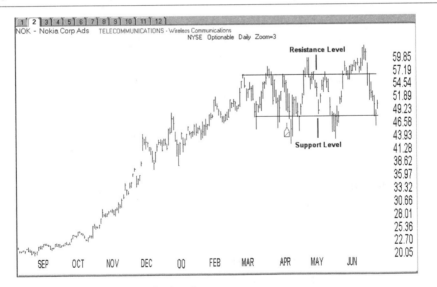

TC2000.com chart courtesy of Worden Brothers, Inc.

figure 3.2 Vignette Corporation (VIGN)

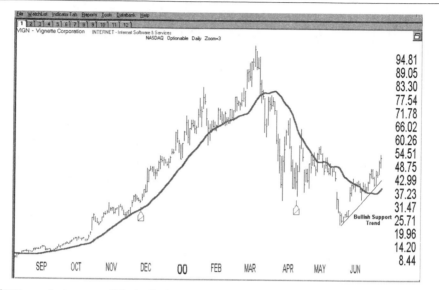

TC2000.com chart courtesy of Worden Brothers, Inc.

figure 3.3 Dell Computer Corp. (DELL)

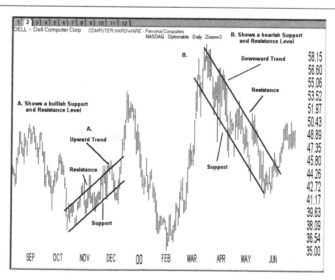

TC2000.com chart courtesy of Worden Brothers, Inc.

then "Trend lines," and "Draw." A more common way to draw trend lines is seen in Figure 3.4. After visually locating your cursor, use the mouse to draw the support line. While it may be just as easy to visualize the Support Level and direction of the stock movement, I've always found it best to draw the support lines. Adding support lines to the chart allows me to properly follow the trend of the stock and execute a trade quickly if needed. To change or erase the support lines, click on "Tools," click on "Trend lines," "Erase," and then "Last one or all" trend lines. Figure 3.5 shows an example. By clicking on "last" you'll only erase the last trend line drawn; clicking on "all" erases all the trend lines for that particular chart. Support Levels have always been great technical indicators as to whether a stock or index can sustain the sell-off created by the downward movement.

How should you react to the Support Level? Investors determine this when deciding to either buy or sell a position. Support Levels can be good indicators for investors to enter a bullish position and buy call options or the stock. Once a stock or index has broken

figure 3.4   Cisco Systems Inc. (CSCO)

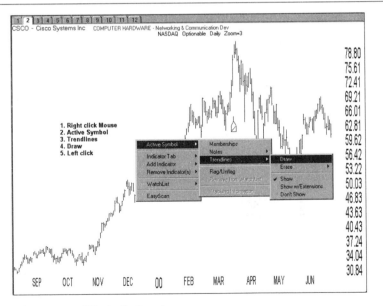

TC2000.com chart courtesy of Worden Brothers, Inc.

figure 3.5   Cisco Systems Inc. (CSCO)

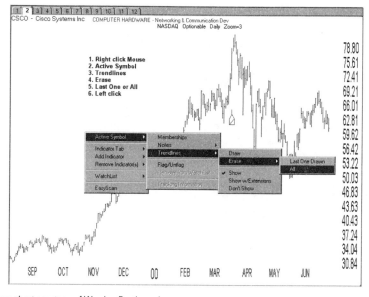

TC2000.com chart courtesy of Worden Brothers, Inc.

below its strongest Support Level, it may be time for investors to exit their trade and take their profits or, just as important, limit their loss with a stop-loss order. Don't allow intraday levels to play a major part on the Support Level unless the overall market is selling off. For instance, if the Support Level of XYZ stock is at $50 and during the market hours the stock drops below $50, I would watch it closely with a stop-loss order but would not exit the trade unless the stock was below $50 after the close of the market. Remember, certain stocks follow certain indexes, which means that if XYZ was a Dow Jones stock and the Dow Jones was selling off, I might play it safe and exit the position.

No question about it, Support Levels do help investors make better-educated decisions. Figures 3.6 and 3.7 present two different charts and time frames showing exactly how the stock reacted after breaking below its Support Level. After a stock or index has dropped below its Support Level, the falling can continue until it reestablishes a new Support Level or crosses back up above its past Support Level.

figure 3.6   CMGI Inc. (CMGI)

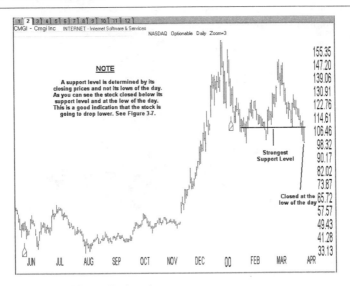

TC2000.com chart courtesy of Worden Brothers, Inc.

figure 3.7   CMGI Inc. (CMGI)

TC2000.com chart courtesy of Worden Brothers, Inc.

As the saying goes on Wall Street, "No one knows how high a stock/index can go up, but by looking at a past chart we can determine how low a stock/index can drop."

Resistance Levels

Resistance Levels are the opposite of Support Levels, being a price level in which a stock may have difficulty moving higher in value. This is commonly caused by the availability of a large supply of stock for sale. Due to the number of shares available, the stock may stop its upward movement and show some signs of a turnaround in a downward direction. Educated investors know that all stocks testing a Resistance Level can show signs of several downward corrections before they break up through a Resistance Level. It is good business to take your profits and stand on the sidelines until the stock/index has proven that the Resistance Level has now become a strong Support Level.

When a stock or index tests a Resistance Level, the only thing that will help it break through that level is good news. Examples of a breakthrough could be because of a strong bullish Dow Jones or Nasdaq Index, good earnings reports, a lower unemployment report, or any positive news about the stock, the economy, or interest rates. As good business practice I have always closed out my bullish positions when a stock hits a new Resistance Level unless my research indicates a possible stock split or my indicators show a continued bullish run. In any case, once the stock reaches a Resistance Level, be sure you limit your downside by placing a stop-loss order.

It may come to a surprise to many investors reading this book, but I'd rather take a bearish position when a stock tests new Resistance Levels than hold a bullish position. History has proven that more often than not, a stock will drop back down to its past Support Level before breaking the higher levels of its resistance. When taking a bearish position, shorting stock (selling at the higher price and buying back at the lower price), or buying put options (your option value increases as the stock value drops), I can generate a profit as the stock/index drops below its past Support Level. The farther the stock drops, the more profits I realize. Figures 3.8 and 3.9 show perfect chart patterns of stocks that tested their Resistance Levels only

figure 3.8   Worldcom Inc. (WCOM)

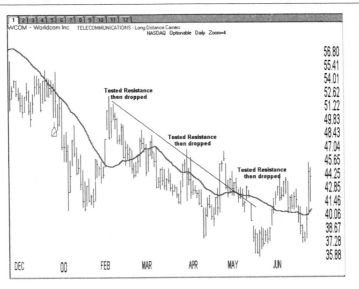

TC2000.com chart courtesy of Worden Brothers, Inc.

figure 3.9   Lucent Technologies Inc. (LU)

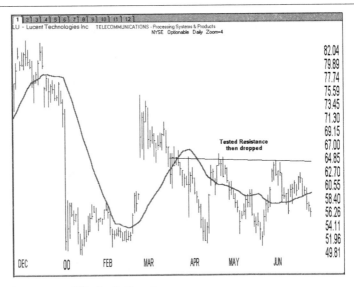

TC2000.com chart courtesy of Worden Brothers, Inc.

to retrace downward to their past Support Levels. Once again, making money on Wall Street is based on education and knowledge of how to react regardless of the overall market condition or an individual stock's direction. Wise investors take profits in both bullish and bearish market conditions.

technical tip

Be very cautious of round numbers. Investors have discovered that stock and/or index prices often find Support or Resistance Levels at round numbers, such as $5, $10, $20, $35, $40, $50, $75, $100, $110, and so on. It is very rare to see a Support or Resistance Level at such odd price levels as $13, $27, $41, $59, $63, $99, $107, and the like. Figures 3.10, 3.11, and 3.12 all show great examples of Support and Resistance Levels at round numbers. Round numbers act as psychological levels that can stop advances or declines. For example, the 10,500 level on the Dow Jones Industrial Average (Figure 3.13) offered resis-

figure 3.10   Amazon.com Inc. (AMZN)

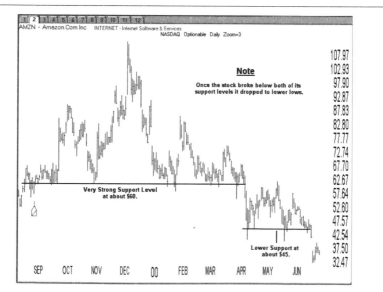

TC2000.com chart courtesy of Worden Brothers, Inc.

figure 3.11 Realnetworks Inc. (RNWK)

TC2000.com chart courtesy of Worden Brothers, Inc.

figure 3.12 Dell Computer Corp. (DELL)

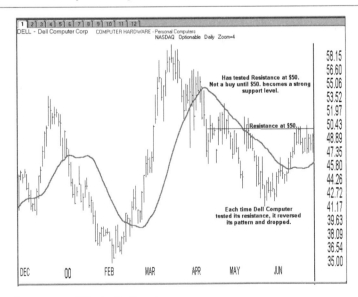

TC2000.com chart courtesy of Worden Brothers, Inc.

figure 3.13   Dow Jones Industrials (DJ-30)

TC2000.com chart courtesy of Worden Brothers, Inc.

tance before it was penetrated. Once the 10,500 level was penetrated, the 10,500 level then became the new Support Level. If the Dow Jones Industrial Average was to drop below the 10,500 Support Level (Figure 3.14), what will the next Support Level be? Another example was the Nasdaq Composite as it tested the Resistance Level of 5,000. The difference between these two Resistance Levels is the simple fact that the stronger of the two indexes is the Dow Jones Industrial Average as its Resistance Level became its new Support Level. The Nasdaq Composite (Figure 3.15) didn't remain above the 5,000 level for long before it retraced its way back down to a new Support Level of 3,800 and then down to the 3,000 level.

Resistance Levels take longer to penetrate and are slower to increase. Support Levels tend to have a shorter penetration period and tend to decrease faster. Round numbers will be of great help not only in determining Support and Resistance Levels, but in helping you determine your entry or exit points. As a market rule, investors don't place trading orders or protective stop-loss orders at round numbers. In an

figure 3.14 Dow Jones Industrials (DJ-30)

TC2000.com chart courtesy of Worden Brothers, Inc.

figure 3.15 Nasdaq Composite Index (COMPQX)

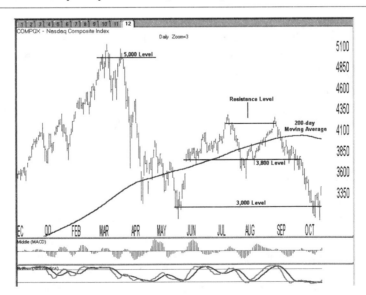

TC2000.com chart courtesy of Worden Brothers, Inc.

upward trend, it is best to place buy orders just above the round numbers and stop-loss orders just below round numbers. To do this, investors use limit orders when buying or selling equities. As a rule of thumb, always know why you bought an equity and, more important, when you will be selling. Round support and resistance numbers will help you make better-educated investment decisions.

Support and Resistance reversal

A reversal is when the Support Level becomes the new Resistance Level, or a new Resistance Level becomes the Support Level, or the Resistance Level becomes the Support Level. Examples of this pattern are shown in Figures 3.16 and 3.17. Notice in Figure 3.18 how during an upward trend the Resistance Level becomes the new Support Level. And in a downward trend, as shown in Figure 3.19, the opposite occurs, as you can see the Resistance Level in a downward trend. When these levels are reversed, it is known as a role reversal. The Support Level becomes the Resistance Level or the Resistance Level becomes the

figure 3.16 Bouygues Offshore Sa Ads (BWG)

TC2000.com chart courtesy of Worden Brothers, Inc.

figure 3.17   Coca-Cola Co. (KO)

TC2000.com chart courtesy of Worden Brothers, Inc.

figure 3.18   Vignette Corporation (VIGN)

TC2000.com chart courtesy of Worden Brothers, Inc.

figure 3.19 Sun Microsystems Inc. (SUNW)

TC2000.com chart courtesy of Worden Brothers, Inc.

Support Level. The likelihood of a role reversal, from support to resistance or resistance to support, depends on several factors. One factors is that the greater the trading volume is at a Support or Resistance Level, the more significant the Support or Resistance Level will be. For example, if XYZ stock is testing a strong Support Level at $50 and the volume on the buying side (known as the ask price) continues to increase, this would be a sign that there are more buyers than sellers and the likelihood of the stock rising in value is good. However, if the Support Level is $50 and the volume on the bid side is greater, this would be an indication that there are more sellers than buyers and the stock may drop below the Support Level of $50.

Another factor is the longer a stock or index trades at its Support or Resistance Level, the greater the chances are for the stock to reverse its role. For example, when a stock/index trades at or near its Resistance Level for several weeks, it will more often than not reverse its trend to a downward bearish movement. Figure 3.20 shows a chart where the stock tested its Resistance Level but couldn't penetrate through, which then created a reversal pattern from a bullish

figure 3.20   CMGI Inc. (CMGI)

TC2000.com chart courtesy of Worden Brothers, Inc.

figure 3.21   Check Point Software Tech (CHKP)

TC2000.com chart courtesy of Worden Brothers, Inc.

trend to a bearish trend. Figure 3.21 shows a bullish chart as the stock penetrated through its Resistance Level, which then became its Support Level. As with any charting technique, you can always find additional patterns that can justify when to buy or sell an investment or just to get an overall view of a stock or index's direction. The most important thing to realize about Support and Resistance Levels is that they exist with *every* stock or index, regardless of how the stock is trading—downward, sideways, or upward. Become good at identifying these levels and predicting which direction the next movement will be.

Chapter 3 Quiz

1. Support Levels allow an investor to see a better indication as to what direction a stock/index may be moving next.

    a. true   b. false

2. Both support and resistance levels can be identified when a stock is moving up, sideways, or down.

    a. true   b. false

3. Resistance levels are a point in which a stock tests new highs and will then begin to drop in value before increasing again.

    a. true   b. false

4. Support and resistance levels both are commonly used in the industry. Of the two, which can have the larger effect on a stock/index?

    a. Support Level   b. resistance level

5. A stock/index that breaks through its resistance level can be considered as:

    a. bearish   b. bullish

6. A stock/index that continuously tests a certain level before changing its direction is an indication of a:

    a. rollover   b. breakout   c. reversal

7. When a stock breaks below its strongest Support Level, the stock can continue to drop until it tests a previous Support Level or establishes a new one.

    a. true   b. false

8. Is it important to check stock volume once the stock crosses above its resistance level?

    a. yes   b. doesn't matter   c. no

9. As a stock goes above its Support Level, it is a good opportunity to buy the stock.

    a. true   b. false

10. Can support and resistance levels be found on such indexes as the Dow Jones Industrial Average and the Nasdaq Composite?

    a. yes   b. no

Chapter 3 Quiz Answers

1. *True*. By identifying a Support Level, you're able to get a better idea if the stock is going to be moving up or down in price.

2. *True*. Support and resistance levels can be seen in stocks that move in all three directions, up, sideways, and down. Figures 3.1, 3.2, and 3.3 show good examples.

3. *True*. Most stocks/indexes that test a resistance level will change directions and drop in value. If the stock has reached these levels before, it may break through and continue a bullish move. Good news will also help a stock/index break through its resistance level onto new highs.

4. Both a support and resistance level have an effect on stocks and indexes, but it's the *Support Level* that investors pay more attention to because it's the "unknown" of not knowing how far down the stock/index can drop after breaking below its Support Level.

5. Stocks/indexes that break above their resistance level will normally be considered a good sign of a *bullish* upward movement.

6. A *reversal* is when a stock/index tests its support or resistance levels and then changes its direction.

7. *True*. When a stock breaks below its Support Level, it will continue to drop until it tests an old Support Level or creates a new one. Be cautious. Many investors are quick to react, thinking that they're buying the stock at a discount, only to find out that they could have bought the stock even lower.

8. *Yes*, it is very important to check a stock's daily volume when it crosses above its resistance level. A crossover with low volume can be a false signal as the stock may quickly do a reversal and drop below the resistance level. This commonly occurs when market makers/specialists who are trying to sell their inventory raise the price to entice investors.

9. *False*. Never assume that just because a stock crosses up over its Support Level it is the perfect time to invest. Allow

the stock to test the Support Level and check other technical indicators, such as the Moving Average and Time Segmented Volume. By doing so you will have a better idea if it's time to buy or be patient.

10. *Yes.* Both the support and resistance levels are found on the indexes as well as individual stocks. The indexes' support and resistance levels are even more common as they test milestone numbers, such as the Dow Jones 10,000 level and the Nasdaq Composite 5,000 level. At times these numbers were both support and resistance levels.

chapter 4

Relative Strength

Relative Strength analysis is an easy concept to understand. It simply compares the performance of one stock with an item such as an industry group of stocks. The objective is to determine if the stock price is advancing or declining faster than the second item. In other words, is the first item (stock) outperforming or underperforming the second item (industry group of stocks) on a relative basis? Relative Strength can be used to compare any two items as long as they each have prices.

individual stock vs. an industry group

It is extremely important to properly research an individual stock to ensure that it is going to offer the greatest return. Many investors don't take time to compare one stock to others in the same business. When utilizing Relative Strength analysis, investors can research an individual stock's performance against the performance of those of the same business. Simply put, if I were to invest in a computer company that built and sold computers, prior to investing I would compare that company's stock against the sector itself to check its overall performance against those in the same business. As investors we all understand that during certain times certain businesses do better than others. The stock market is no different than children's toys at

Christmas time. Each year a new toy comes out that every child on the block must own. The interest for the hottest toy creates an increase in demand, which ultimately creates an increase in the toy's value. The day after Christmas the toy's value drops as the demand drops. Yet on Christmas, if you tried to explain to your child that you bought another toy instead of the hottest toy, you would have a very dissatisfied child. The same with the stock market. Certain stocks within certain sectors (businesses) create more interest than others. Select the most favorable stock based on a comparison of how it performs against all other stocks in that same business. Select stocks that are moving in the same direction as the industry group.

individual stocks vs. certain indexes

Just as important, investors compare individual stocks to the overall performance of indexes such as the Dow Jones Industrial Average (Dow), Nasdaq Composite (COMPQX), or the Standard & Poor's 500 Index (S&P 500). When comparing a stock with an index, investors gain a better understanding as to how an individual stock/index moves with other stocks or indexes. I've made it good practice to compare Internet stocks to the Nasdaq Composite, as most Internet stocks tend to move up or down with the movement of the Nasdaq Composite. Figure 4.1 shows an example of Yahoo! Inc. (YHOO) being compared to the Nasdaq Composite. As you can see, both the Nasdaq Composite and YHOO move together and on a longer-term chart YHOO has outperformed the Nasdaq. Figure 4.2 shows an overall bearish movement by both Procter & Gamble and the Dow Jones Industrial. Once a stock can't keep up with the index or industry group, you may want to consider investing in something else. Procter & Gamble did have bad news but since that time it has continued to underperform the Dow Jones Index.

industry groups vs. indexes

Investors compare industry groups to the market as a whole using Relative Strength analysis to determine which industry groups are outperforming or underperforming the overall market. Investors commonly use these indicators to help them select certain groups that may or may not be affected by the overall market condition of the

figure 4.1 Yahoo! Inc. (YHOO)

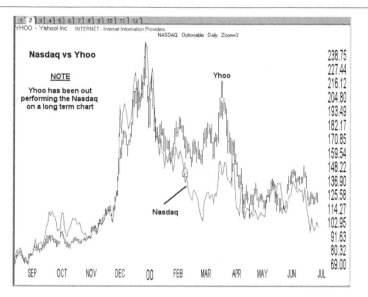

TC2000.com chart courtesy of Worden Brothers, Inc.

figure 4.2 Procter & Gamble Co. (PG)

TC2000.com chart courtesy of Worden Brothers, Inc.

selected index. Bullish investors would select an industry group of stocks that move in an upward direction with a bullish index. On the other side are industry stocks that move downward in a bearish market as the index moves downward. Being able to trade with the direction of the market enables investors to make money in both a bullish and a bearish market. It's easy to select a bullish stock in a bullish market or a bearish stock in a bearish market. Using Relative Strength comparison enables investors to select the sector that is moving the greatest amount, which provides them with more opportunity.

You'll note that I refer to both outperforming and underperforming; it's important to invest in both bullish upward markets and bearish downward markets. Again, many investors always invest long. Yet during certain times you'd want to invest in bearish stocks or markets. If you are not investing in bearish markets, I assure you your broker and mutual funds are. The word "underperforming" is so rarely used that the spell check on my new computer doesn't even recognize the word. Yet as a full-time investor, I've realized good returns by shorting stocks/indexes or buying put options on individual stocks or indexes that are trading in a downward motion.

technical analysis tip

Investors follow a certain format to select the right industry group and then the right stock. First they determine which industry groups are outperforming the overall market (if they're looking to be bullish) or underperforming the overall market (if they're looking to be bearish). Then they determine which stocks in the highest-ranking industry groups are outperforming (if bullish) or underperforming (if bearish) the industry group. Finally, they use various technical analysis tools (i.e., chart patterns, Balance of Power, MoneyStream, Moving Averages, etc.) to find the right entry point. Never forget the Wall Street saying, "The trend is your friend." Even if the Relative Strength of a stock is strong, be sure to check other various technical analyses to determine if the market is in an upward trend or a downtrend to assure a good entry point. Remember, if the Relative Strength is very high (bullish) and the overall market is trending down, the odds are the stock will drop as well. There may be a better opportunity if you took a bearish position and shorted/bought puts or stood on the sideline. Stocks move in the direction of the overall market. Thus, if you invest with the market direction and not against it, the trend is your friend.

Follow these steps to add Relative Strength to your chart. First, move your cursor onto the section of the chart where you want to add the Relative Strength (top, versus middle or bottom). In this example we will be adding Relative Strength to the top price chart. Right-click on your mouse, go to "Add indicator," find Relative Strength, then single click with the left mouse button (see Figure 4.3). At this point decide which part of the chart you want Relative Strength added to (top). Once you have the top selected, you may left-click OK (see Figure 4.4). You should now be in the white and gray editing indicator tab box shown in Figure 4.5 (be sure you have the Prices–Bar Chart). Left-click the gray change box located in the upper right corner, and type in the RS Symbol (comparison symbol for the group you're comparing the stock against). Figure 4.6 compares the Relative Strength of Wal-Mart (WMT) to the Dow Jones Industrial Average (DJ-30). So we add the symbol DJ-30 in the RS Symbol.

Special note: If you don't know the index or industry group symbols, you can find them by looking under the different categories lo-

figure 4.3   Wal-Mart Stores Inc. (WMT)

TC2000.com chart courtesy of Worden Brothers, Inc.

figure 4.4   Wal-Mart Stores Inc. (WMT)

TC2000.com chart courtesy of Worden Brothers, Inc.

figure 4.5   Wal-Mart Stores Inc. (WMT)

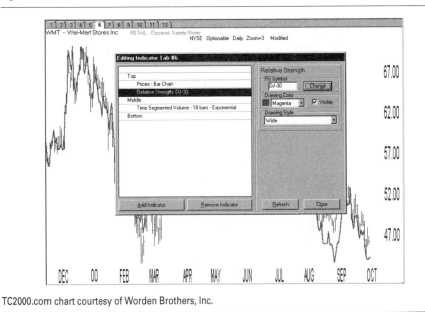

TC2000.com chart courtesy of Worden Brothers, Inc.

figure 4.6 Wal-Mart Stores Inc. (WMT)

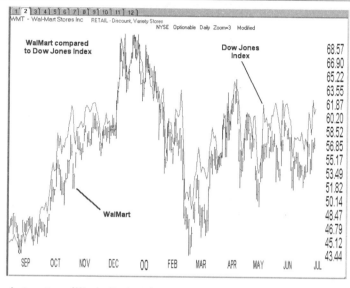

TC2000.com chart courtesy of Worden Brothers, Inc.

cated in the upper left corner of the chart under the heading Watch-List. Change the watch list to your selected category. For instance, in this example I'd change the watch list to "All Indexes." There I will find the symbol DJ-30 for the Dow Jones Industrial Average. After adding the DJ-30 symbol, select your color and then be sure you've selected the visible box. Finally decide what kind of drawing style you'd like to appear on the chart (normal, wide, dashed, and dotted).

You are now able to compare the Relative Strength of one stock to another stock. (Figure 4.7 compares the Relative Strength of Home Depot to Wal-Mart.) Comparing Home Depot to Wal-Mart gives an investor a better indication of which stock is performing better than the other. Stocks vs. indexes (Figure 4.8 compares Wal-Mart to the Dow 30) compares the Dow stock Wal-Mart to the entire performance of the Dow Jones Industrial Average. Is WMT moving up or down with DJ-30? A positive upward movement of the Dow and a bearish downward movement of Wal-Mart may not be a good time to buy Wal-Mart. Positive index and stock are a bullish sign. See stocks vs. industry groups (Figure 4.9 compares Wal-Mart to the retail sector) or any other ver-

figure 4.7 Wal-Mart Stores Inc. (WMT)

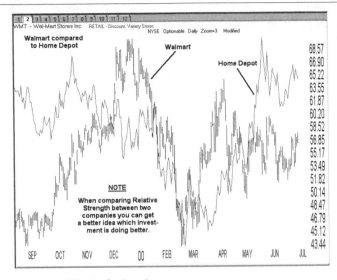

TC2000.com chart courtesy of Worden Brothers, Inc.

figure 4.8 Wal-Mart Stores Inc. (WMT)

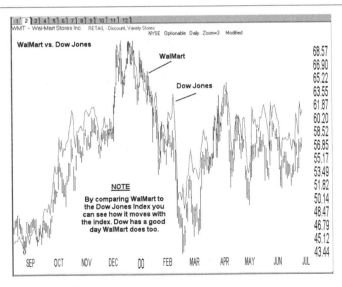

TC2000.com chart courtesy of Worden Brothers, Inc.

figure 4.9   Wal-Mart Stores Inc. (WMT)

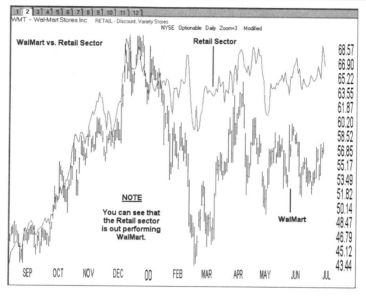

TC2000.com chart courtesy of Worden Brothers, Inc.

sion, such as industry groups vs. industry groups, or industry groups vs. indexes.

Remember, the purpose of comparing any two items is to look at the overall chart to see how one item may be outperforming another if you are going to be bullish or underperforming another item if you are going to be bearish. The overall market or sector trend is important, yet by utilizing the Relative Strength indicators, you are able to pick and choose investments that outperform others or, more important, that aren't as volatile and sensitive to market swings as others may be.

Chapter 4 Quiz

1. Relative Strength indicators are used to compare a stock or index with which of the following?
   a. another stock   b. an index   c. a sector   d. all three

2. In order for Relative Strength to work properly, the two items being compared must have large price and volume movements.
   a. true   b. false

3. Using Relative Strength indicators can help locate stocks that are moving in the opposite direction of the market trend.
   a. true   b. false

4. The main purpose of comparing two items against each other is to identify the ideal time to buy or sell an investment.
   a. true   b. false

5. The S&P 500 index cannot be compared to the Nasdaq Composite.
   a. true   b. false

6. It's best to consider a bullish or bearish investment after you've checked the industry/index group of the individual stock you are investing in.
   a. true   b. false

7. Select individual stocks that are moving the same direction as their industry group.
   a. true   b. false

8. Relative Strength can be used only when making bullish investments.
   a. true   b. false

9. Market trends (up or down) can affect the direction of a stock regardless of the Relative Strength indicator.
   a. true   b. false

10. If you're unsure of an index or industry symbol, you can find it by looking where?
    a. sector list   b. WatchList   c. group symbols

Chapter 4 Quiz Answers

1. The answer is *all three*. Relative Strength is used to compare data to data; we can compare stocks to stocks, stocks to indexes, stocks to sectors, or any other combination.

2. *False.* A stock doesn't have to have large volume. Relative Strength is an indicator that is based on price movement.

3. *True.* Relative Strength can be used to give an investor an idea of which stocks are performing the opposite of the market.

4. *False.* Relative Strength is commonly used to compare a stock or index to other stocks or indexes to determine a bullish or bearish comparison.

5. *False.* The S&P 500 Index and the Nasdaq Composite can be compared to each other to get a better understanding as to which stocks within certain indexes are performing better.

6. *True.* When investing in either a bullish or a bearish movement, confirm the movement of the index/industry group before choosing the proper investment.

7. *True.* The stronger the index/industry group is, the better the individual movement of the stock may be. This also applies to bearish investments; the stronger the decrease in the sector, the stronger the bearish investment could be.

8. *False.* Relative Strength is commonly used in both bullish and bearish investments.

9. *True.* The overall market direction can affect an individual investment. Invest long in a bullish trend and short in a bearish trend.

10. To find an index/industry group symbol, you can use the *WatchList* file of TC2000.

chapter 5

Balance of Power

Balance of Power (or BOP, for short) is the exclusive intellectual property of Worden Brothers, Inc., which means that it can be found only with their TC2000® program. It was developed many years ago by Don Worden, a leading technical innovator and writer. Because it dates back many years, this technical tool can provide investors with a proven record of its value. A simple explanation of the BOP technical indicator is "large volume of stock being bought or sold."

What separates Balance of Power from the many other indicators used today is the fact that its indicator signals are made up of a stock's individual volume movement and the price movement. Two other technical indicators made up of the stock's volume movement and price movement are MoneyStream and Time Segmented Volume (or TSV). Because these indicators concern both the stock's volume (buying and selling) and its price, investors tend to feel that they have an advantage over other indicators. Both MoneyStream and Time Segmented Volume are described elsewhere in this book. Getting back to Balance of Power, let's review why such an indicator that uses volume movement with price movement is of importance to investors.

First, investors need to always remember the important rule that just because a stock has increased in value doesn't necessarily mean that more stock was bought than sold at that time. Figure 5.1 shows an

figure 5.1   Procter & Gamble Co. (PG)

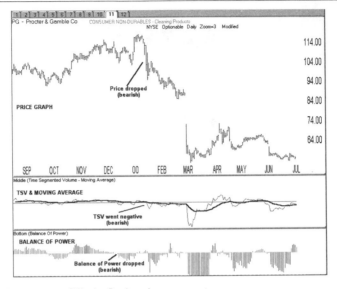

TC2000.com chart courtesy of Worden Brothers, Inc.

example (before) of a stock that has a strong price pattern yet the BOP shows the stock as being overbought. Figure 5.2 shows the after-effect of the stock as the price chart looked positive yet the BOP and TSV indicators showed the stock being sold. The outcome of the BOP indicator would have limited investors' losses as the stock dropped from approximately $70 per share down to approximately $50 per share and then even lower. The theory of supply and demand can dictate the direction of a stock's movement; if an individual stock has greater demand than stock available, then it will tend to increase in value as more investors buy it.

The same theory applies to a stock that has a greater supply available with less demand; the stock may have a tendency to decrease in value. Yet we as investors must always remember that stocks are controlled by market makers (Nasdaq) and specialists (Dow Jones) whose responsibility is to make a market for the stock. They do this by controlling the number of shares traded between a willing buyer and a willing seller. It's because of market makers and specialists that we as investors need not only technical indicators to assist us but technical indicators that are based on the total daily

figure 5.2   Procter & Gamble Co. (PG)

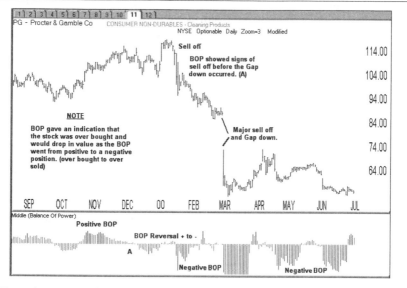

TC2000.com chart courtesy of Worden Brothers, Inc.

trading volume. As an investor I like to know whether a stock was overbought or oversold during a particular day or the last several days. Think about it; say you are looking to buy a stock, and the past several days or weeks there has been excessive buying, causing the price to run up. Now large investors are considering selling the stock. You may just have bought at the wrong time, as the stock could have been overbought and now is on its way down.

ECNs are often used to buy or sell stock while hiding identity. An ECN is none other than a broker who will do business with any investor by allowing that investor (individual or firm) to execute trades through the electronic communication network (ECN). So how does this affect the average investor? ECNs such as All-Tech (ATTN), Instinet (INCA), Small Order Execution System (SOES), and Island (ISLD) are in business for the same reasons you and I are: to make money. A small or large investor can buy or sell stocks or options using different ECNs.

Investors using ECNs have three advantages. First, their identity is not revealed to the market because only the ECN's identity appears on the screen. Investors are unable to see that the seller is, for example, a very well known brokerage firm or fund manager who is unloading an investment in anticipation of the stock taking a large drop. A good example of this occurred with the well-known Nasdaq stock Rambus Inc. (RMBS). Figure 5.3 shows a great example of the sell-off. Figure 5.4 shows an Attain/RealTick Level 2 screen listing a few of the ECNs and brokerage firms that were buying and selling RMBS.

Second, ECNs give investors the ability to trade before and after normal market hours. Thus they can take part of positive or negative news before the average investor.

And third, but most important, ECNs enable investors to hide not only their identity but also the number of shares they're buying or selling. The ability to utilize ECNs allows investors to continuously buy or sell stock in smaller increments, so they do not alarm the market that they are looking to unload, for example, a large amount of one particular stock. Figure 5.5 shows an example of a stock that was sold continuously for two weeks in increments of only 100 shares at a time. If the broker was to sell 500,000 shares of stock at one time, the stock price would drop much faster. The broker wouldn't be able to maximize profits as the stock price was decreasing in value. Balance of Power allows me to have a better indication as to whether the stock

figure 5.3   Rambus Inc. (RMBS)

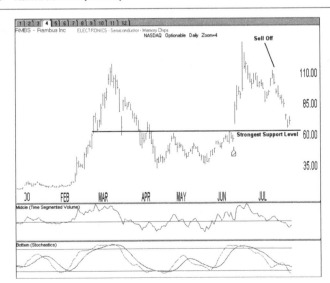

TC2000.com chart courtesy of Worden Brothers, Inc.

figure 5.4 Rambus, Inc. (RMBS)

RAMBUS, INC.						
RMBS	70 7/8	↑ -2 7/16	400	US Q 11:04		
High 74 7/16	Low	70 1/8	Acc. Vol. 1414100			
Bid ↓ 70 13/16	Ask	70 15/16	Close	73 5/16		

Name	Bid	Size	Name	Ask	Size	
ISLD	70 13/16	*ECN 1	NITE	70 15/16	1	
MWSE	70 3/4	8	REDI	70 15/16	5	
NEUB	70 3/4	1	BRUT	70 15/16	1	
NFSC	70 3/4	1	ISLD	71	*ECN 1	
INCA	70 3/4	*ECN 5	PERT	71 1/8	1	
FLTT	70 1/2	1	MWSE	71 1/4	6	
BRUT	70 1/2	2	INCA	71 1/4	*ECN 2	
MASH	70 1/2	1	MLCO	71 1/2	1	
NITE	70 3/8	1	MASH	71 1/2	5	
SLKC	70 5/16	1	FLTT	71 3/4	1	
ARCA	70 1/4	*ECN 5	CWCO	71 7/8	1	
PERT	70 1/4	2	HMQT	72	1	
REDI	70 1/4	2	NEUB	72	1	
PFSI	70 1/8	1	PFSI	72 1/16	1	
HRZG	70 1/16	1	BTRD	72 1/16	1	
JEFF	70	1	SLKC	72 1/16	1	
CANT	70	1	COWN	72 1/4	1	
PIPR	70	1	PIPR	72 1/4	1	
SBSH	70	2	MONT	72 5/8	1	
MLCO	70	2	SBSH	72 5/8	1	
LEHM	69 3/4	1	RSSF	72 3/4	1	
INGC	69 11/16	1	ARCA	72 3/4	5	
MSCO	69 1/4	1	NFSC	72 13/16	1	
JOSE	69	1	AAWC	73	5	
SNDS	69	1	HRZG	73	3	
WARR	68 3/4	1	BEST	73 1/2	1	
RAMS	68 1/4	1	SHWD	74 1/2	1	
COWN	00 1/4	1	LEHM	74 1/2	1	
MONT	68 3/16	1	COST	74 1/2	2	
HMQT	68 1/8	1	INGC	74 11/16	1	
BEST	68	5	SNDS	74 11/16	1	
SHWD	67 3/8	1	CANT	75	1	
FCAP	67 3/8	1	MSCO	75 3/8	1	
OLDE	67	2	WARR	75 7/16	1	
COST	67	2	FCAP	75 1/2	1	
RSSF	65 3/4	1	JOSE	76	1	

Chart provided by Attain/RealTick.

was being overbought or oversold. Reviewing Figure 5.5 you'll notice the negative BOP indicating the selling of the stock. The price found a Support Level and turned around only to drop down again. This example is only one of many that give investors false signals. Figure 5.6 shows an example of a price bar chart (top), Time Segmented Volume with Moving Average (middle), and Balance of Power (bottom). The ability to add additional technical indicators has great value. In this example the price bar chart looked promising but the BOP and Moving Average indicated more selling to come.

Truly, Balance of Power allows an investor to predetermine whether a stock is being bought (accumulated) or sold (distributed).

figure 5.5 Davox Corp. (DAVX)

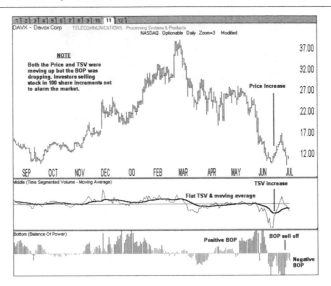

TC2000.com chart courtesy of Worden Brothers, Inc.

figure 5.6 Davox Corp. (DAVX)

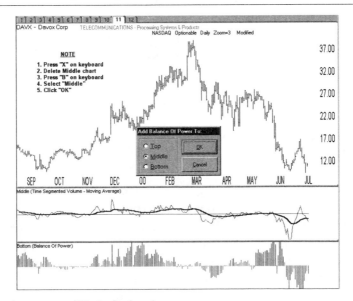

TC2000.com chart courtesy of Worden Brothers, Inc.

This enables investors an opportunity to predetermine the movement of a stock's bullish (upward) or bearish (downward) movement. To add Balance of Power as an indicator, you must first press the X key on your keyboard, allowing you to delete your old technical indicators. Figure 5.7 shows you how to add BOP to your current selected indicators. After deleting your old indicators, you can press the B key to access the BOP window. Figure 5.8 shows you how to properly set up your Balance of Power indicators. Balance of Power operates from what is known as a level line, an imaginary line that runs horizontally through the middle of the screen from left to right. The level line is an indication point at which a stock is being bullish, neutral, or bearish.

It's said that accumulated green BOP can be an indication of the stock being bullish, as the volume increases as more stock is being bought than what is being sold. The yellow BOP indicates that the stock is in a neutral pattern with uncertain direction of buying or selling. And the red BOP indicates that the stock is being bearish, as more stock is being sold than bought. By watching the green, yellow, and red volume indicators, investors can learn whether a stock is showing a change in pattern or direction. Balance of Power enables investors

figure 5.7   Davox Corp. (DAVX)

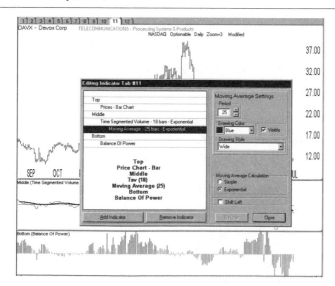

TC2000.com chart courtesy of Worden Brothers, Inc.

figure 5.8   Apple Computer Inc. (AAPL)

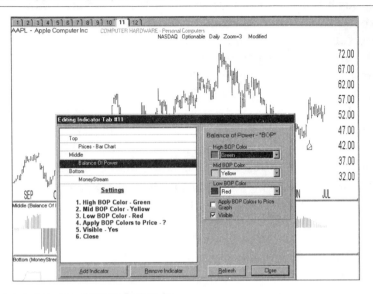

TC2000.com chart courtesy of Worden Brothers, Inc.

to make educated investments by anticipating what the stock's next direction may be. Remember the saying on Wall Street, "The trend is your friend." More selling than buying can cause a stock to drop in value; more buying than selling can cause a stock to increase in value.

A stock's trend can be based on either buying or selling volume. What most investors need to understand is that large trades (normally 10,000 shares plus) can create an increase or a decrease in an individual stock's value. The larger the stock's daily volume, the smaller the impact will be; the larger the stock's daily volume, the smaller the impact can be. For example, referring to Cisco (CSCO), a trade of 10,000 shares may not affect the price when its daily volume is in excess of 34 million shares. However, an investor buying or selling 100,000 shares can affect price movement. Any time a block trade is made, market makers/specialists will adjust the price of the stock for their benefit.

Stocks that follow an upward trend yet show a yellow neutral BOP should put the investors on alert because the yellow accumulation at the zero line could be a sign that the stock buying is drying up. It also can be the beginning of a turnaround as the BOP drops below the level line, creating a change in the stock's character and price. A dry-up of buying may be a strong bearish sign, as the stock will show increasing yellow or red BOP below the level line. A true bearish signal is normally confirmed when the BOP drops below the level line and the stock price drops in conjunction with the BOP. The reduction of both the stock price and BOP will alert investors to close out their long position and/or take on a short position. A perfect example of this was shown with Procter & Gamble (PG) in Figures 5.1 and 5.2.

Bullish price increases along with strong green BOP accumulation can be a great opportunity to take a long position (buy stock or call options). A bullish signal is when the green Balance of Power is to the plus side of the level line as the price level increases and the green BOP rises higher above the level line. When using BOP indicators, remember not to be misled thinking that a stock is going up in value just because the BOP indicator goes from the negative level line or neutral position above the level line. Stocks that show strong BOP signs can change direction rather rapidly; always check other indicators and never rely on just one technical indicator. Checking a stock's support and Resistance Level of the past price movement can also help identify or confirm the direction of its movement. If you're viewing a stock that is showing a lot of green accumulation on the BOP indicator and the stock's price movement is testing a Resistance Level, wait for the stock to confirm the bullish movement by breaking through that Resistance Level. Many investors are quick to act (buy) when taking a long position once the BOP and price have moved up, yet the stock can quickly change its direction if it doesn't break through its Resistance Level. Again, be sure to view the stock's past price pattern and its reaction as it tested its previous Resistance Levels.

The same applies to Support Levels; don't solely rely on the price movement and BOP indicator. Stocks that have broken below their Support Level are not sure investments either; they can have a change of character and suddenly reverse their direction. Regardless of how strong your price movement or Balance of Power indicators are, always remember that a complete overview of several different technical indicators will make you a better investor. The rewards will be better profits and limited losses. The Balance of Power indicator provides you with one more powerful technical indicator as an investor.

Chapter 5 Quiz

1. What color Balance of Power would give a bullish buying signal?

   a. green   b. yellow   c. red

2. What is a good technical indicator used with BOP?

   a. MoneyStream   b. Stochastic   c. Moving Average

3. When you see excessive yellow on the BOP, what does this indicate?

   a. overbought   b. neutral   c. oversold

4. Can a stock price increase while the BOP indicator is decreasing?

   a. yes   b. no   c. forgot

5. Which of the following calculates the BOP indicator?

   a. volume   b. price   c. both

6. The bullish signal is noted when the BOP crosses the level line where?

   a. above the level line   b. below the level line

7. When a stock has increased in price and the positive green BOP indicator changes to red, what does this indicate regarding the stock price?

   a. it will continue to go up   b. it may pull back down

8. Investors can rely on the BOP as an entry or exit point of a trade.

   a. true   b. false   c. read the chapter again

9. Stocks that test a Resistance Level and show a positive green BOP are always good stocks to buy.

   a. true   b. false

10. Does a support and Resistance Level play a big part in a stock's movement even if the BOP is positive?

    a. yes   b. no

Chapter 5 Quiz Answers

1. A *green* BOP above the level line offers the best technical indication that a stock is bullish, as at this point there are more buyers than sellers. The yellow BOP can be a bullish signal if the accumulation is above the zero line and the BOP's past pattern is being duplicated.

2. A good technical indicator used with BOP is the *Moving Average*. Moving Average can be overlapped directly on the same chart with the BOP, allowing the investor to select an entry or exit point as the BOP moves above or below its Moving Average.

3. An excessive amount of yellow on a chart is normally a sign that buyers and sellers are *neutral*. The importance of the neutral (yellow) is determined by whether the stock is above or below the level line. Above the level line could still be bullish and below the level line could be bullish. Overall, the yellow BOP indicates that the stock is being bought and sold equally. Look at it as if it were a yellow street signal: "proceed with caution."

4. *Yes.* It is very common for the stock price to increase while the BOP indicators are decreasing. The important thing to remember is that this could be a change of character for the stock as more stock is being sold than being bought. This also could be a good sign that others know more about the stock than you may and are electing to exit the position.

5. The BOP is a proprietary technical indicator that is comprised of *both* the stock's price movement and its volume. It allows investors the ability to react not just on a stock's price movement.

6. The ideal entry point to buy is recognized as the green BOP increases (*above the level line*) to higher highs after changing from red or yellow on the negative side of the level line. If a stock has a previous pattern of not crossing below the level

line, then you'd wait for an increase in the BOP along with an increase in the stock's daily volume.

7. The BOP changing from green to red could be a signal that the stock is experiencing a change of character. It could change from a bullish signal to a bearish signal as the stock may have been overbought.

8. *True.* Understanding how BOP works allows investors more opportunity to elect a better entry or exit point. BOP and other indicators enable knowledgeable investors to make educated trades that aren't based solely on the fundamentals of a stock.

9. *False.* One of the most common mistakes of investors is buying a stock at its 52-week high. Even though a stock has reached a new high and the BOP indicator is aggressively green (positive), view the stock's past to see what its reaction was last time it tested this or another Resistance Level. Most stocks will go into a correction period because they are overbought before breaking the Resistance Level.

10. *Yes.* Support and Resistance Levels can have a major effect on the stock's direction. A stock that is slowly increasing its price and volume has a better chance of breaking up through its Resistance Level. The same applies to a Support Level; if the stock has a slowly decreasing price and volume, it has a better chance of sustaining its Support Level. The largest factor of impact for a support or Resistance Level is news. Good news will move the stock above its Resistance Level; bad news can drive a stock below its Support Level.

chapter 6

Moving Averages

Moving Averages are one of the most widely used tools in today's market. These averages are just another technical tool found within investors' toolboxes. Various types of Moving Averages are used to calculate price movements of a stock or index. Their largest advantage is to help investors get a better understanding of the price trend of a stock or index. The greater the volatility of the market, the greater the demand for the use of Moving Averages. Before discussing various types of Moving Averages, it is important to understand exactly what a Moving Average is.

A Moving Average is the sum of whatever you are examining (e.g., the closing prices of a stock) for a number of days (e.g., seven days), divided by the number of days (e.g., 10 days). A seven-day Moving Average includes yesterday's figures; tomorrow the same average will include today's figures and will no longer show those for the earliest date included in yesterday's average. Thus every day it picks up figures for the last day and drops those for the earliest day. The "moving" part of the Moving Average is just the recalculation of the price average of each day. It is important to know the difference between the several different types of Moving Averages.

simple Moving Average

Many investors use simple Moving Averages, because they are the easiest type of Moving Average to calculate and are reasonably effective. Moving Averages can be used with all different time frames, ranging from minutes to weeks to months. The most commonly known average is 200 days. An investor's trading purpose determines the time frame used to figure an entry and exit point of a trade. Day traders who look to buy and sell within the same day prefer to use a Moving Average of *minutes*, not days. The most common Moving Average when day trading is a two-minute average. The time frame of the Moving Average, two minutes in this example, means that the price is recalculated every two minutes giving a new price average.

The shorter-term position traders use averages of seven and 10 days. And of course longer-term buy and hold investors use a time frame of 20, 50, 100, or 200 days. The purpose of any Moving Average is to assist an investor to know when the proper time to buy or sell an investment is. To calculate an example of a seven-day Moving Average for Nokia (NOK), I've totaled the last seven-day closing prices of $56.06, $59.31, $56.00, $55.56, $56.00, $57.00, and $54.00 totaling $393.93. The next step is to divide the total by the number of days, which in this example is seven days, giving you a Moving Average of $56.27. This represents the average price of the stock over the last seven trading days. The best way to implement your own selected Moving Average is to select a charting software program that does the work for you. Set up your Moving Averages with different time frames, allowing you to view not only individual stocks but also different indexes.

Figure 6.1 shows an example of a Moving Average being added to a Time Segmented Volume. It can also be added to other indicators, such as volume, Balance of Power, Relative Strength, price charts, and others. I prefer to use a simple Moving Average with both a price bar chart and Time Segmented Volume indicators. If using TC2000, the easiest way to adjust the Moving Average for your needs is to right-click within the desired area you're adding the Moving Average to, add indicator, then left-click on Moving Average. At this point the Moving Average Settings box will appear on the screen, as seen in Figure 6.2. The rest of the settings are self-explanatory. You would set the time period (seven days in my example), choose the color of the Moving Average

figure 6.1   Biogen Inc. (BGEN)

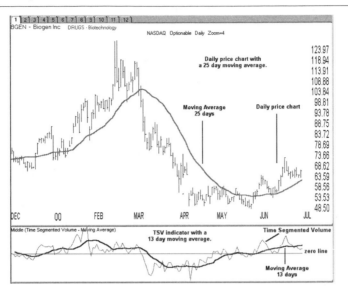

TC2000.com chart courtesy of Worden Brothers, Inc.

figure 6.2   Biogen Inc. (BGEN)

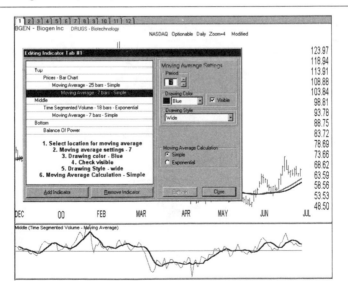

TC2000.com chart courtesy of Worden Brothers, Inc.

indicator (I use cyan), then check the box for simple Moving Average, and finish by refreshing the chart. You now have added a simple Moving Average to the chart of your choice.

Simple Moving Averages are used not only for individual stock charting but can be used to follow different indexes, such as the Dow Jones or Nasdaq Composite. They are heavily used in individual sectors, such as the Internet, computer, drug, retail, and oil industries. The most commonly used Moving Average indicator on Wall Street is the simple 200-day Moving Average of the Dow Jones Industrial Average and the Nasdaq Composite, which are shown in Figures 6.3 and 6.4. As a rule of thumb, as long as the indexes are above the 200-day simple Moving Average, the current outlook is bullish. On the other hand, when an individual stock or index crosses below the 200-day simple Moving Average, it is now becoming bearish. If a stock or index drops below its 200-day Moving Average, it may be a sign of a bearish reaction that can continue much lower. Using the Nasdaq Composite as an example, compare Figure 6.4 to Figure 6.5 and you'll see a perfect example of a bearish movement.

figure 6.3   Dow Jones Industrials (DJ-30)

TC2000.com chart courtesy of Worden Brothers, Inc.

figure 6.4 **Nasdaq Composite Index (COMPQX)**

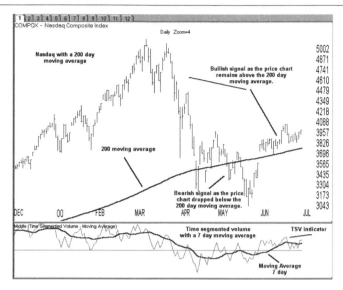

TC2000.com chart courtesy of Worden Brothers, Inc.

figure 6.5 **Nasdaq Composite Index (COMPQX)**

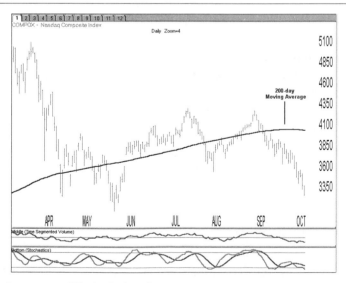

TC2000.com chart courtesy of Worden Brothers, Inc.

Figure 6.4 shows the Nasdaq index at 3,991 and above its 200-day Moving Average. Figure 6.5 shows a bearish correction as the index dropped below the 200-day Moving Average as it was trading down 739 points to 3,252 (739 points is a large bearish correction).

In Chapter 13, I will explain why and how such technical indicators enabled me to change from a bullish investor to a bearish investor.

During bullish markets, investors don't refer to the 200-day Moving Average. They use shorter averages, such as the 100-, 50-, or 20-day Moving Average. I've always found it amazing that so much talk is generated when the markets drop lower to test the 200-day average. If you haven't exited the position much earlier, why even use a Moving Average at all? On the reverse side, the Moving Average can be beneficial when crossing up over the 200-day average, as it can be a bullish sign.

exponential Moving Average

An exponential Moving Average is calculated slightly differently from a simple Moving Average. Exponential Moving Averages are used to get a more responsive movement of the underlying data. When considering which Moving Average would work for you, consider the exponential Moving Average if you're looking for sooner swings more often. Figure 6.6 shows the difference between the two movements. Because exponential Moving Averages are more volatile, they have a tendency to be more active than other Moving Averages, which can lead to false indications. To avoid these false signals, always be sure to compare the Moving Average with other indicators. Don't react immediately just because the Moving Average is moving. Reconfirm your decision and view the simple Moving Average as well. More investors make the wrong decision because they rely just on an exponential Moving Average.

weighted Moving Average

Weighted Moving Averages don't give an equal weighted value to the stock or index. The two common terms used with weighted Moving Averages are front-weighted and back-weighted. With a front-weighted

figure 6.6   Davox Corp. (DAVX)

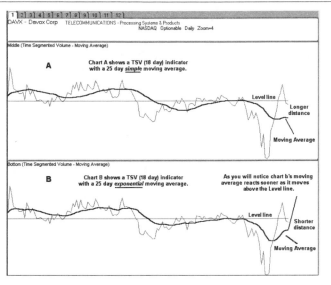

TC2000.com chart courtesy of Worden Brothers, Inc.

average, the Moving Average multiplies each value toward the most recent and current data. The back-weighted average puts more value of the price on the later part of the data. Weighted Moving Averages can also be referred to as leading or lagging indicators.

A lagging indicator is one that follows the market and has a tendency not to change direction until after the stock/index has already done so. The positive aspect of this allows investors not to react too quickly. Lagging indicators are known to follow the direction of the stock/index and not lead. A leading indicator has more of a tendency to react before the stock/index does. Regardless of which type of Moving Average you use, your time frame is of more importance. Longer-term investors use a moving average time frame of about 45 days or longer. Mid-term investors prefer an 18-day moving average. Short-term or day traders rely on the shortest average of minutes. Moving Averages tend to be more accurate when used with trending markets. Figure 6.7 shows an 18-day Moving Average on a price chart. Figure 6.8 shows a 13-day Moving Average on a Time Segmented Volume (TSV) indicator.

figure 6.7   Davox Corp. (DAVX)

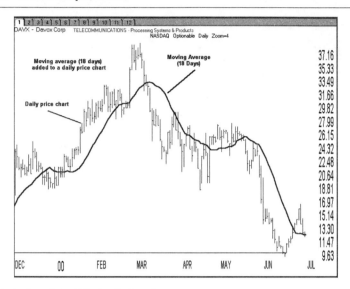

TC2000.com chart courtesy of Worden Brothers, Inc.

figure 6.8   Davox Corp. (DAVX)

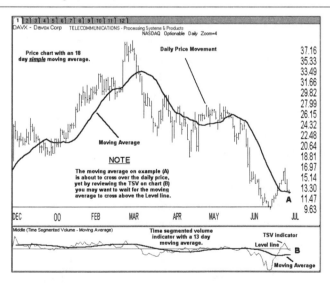

TC2000.com chart courtesy of Worden Brothers, Inc.

By viewing these two charts you'll have a better understanding of what direction the stock may be moving. The price movement remaining above your Moving Average can be a positive sign; once the Moving Average drops below the price, the stock/index may be experiencing a change of direction and become negative. When both the TSV and Moving Average indicator are above the level line, you have a positive signal. Once they cross below the level line, the movement could become a negative signal. As you view both of these charts, also remember that the overall market trend or stock trend plays a heavy role in the stock's movement. If you're looking at stocks that are in a bullish sector, that's a plus to your side if you're buying. But if you're looking to buy a stock within a bearish sector, be careful and review the Moving Average on a shorter seven-day time frame to get a better idea of its short-term outlook or consider a bearish investment.

Chapter 6 Quiz

1. Both a stock's price and volume movement determine the Moving Averages.
   a. true   b. false

2. When using a Moving Average indicator as a long-term investor, it's best to use which one of the three time frames?
   a. short   b. medium   c. long

3. A Moving Average that has a tendency to be more volatile with larger movements more often is known as:
   a. simple   b. exponential   c. weighted

4. When using the term "front-loaded" or "back-loaded," an investor is using which Moving Average?
   a. weighted   b. exponential   c. simple

5. Many investors consider the overall market condition to be bearish when the simple Moving Average of the Dow Jones Industrial crosses below which Moving Average?
   a. 50-day   b. 100-day   c. 200-day

6. A Moving Average can be added to other technical indicators as a way of weighting the movement of that particular indicator.
   a. true   b. false

7. Moving Averages can be recalculated as often as every minute.
   a. true   b. false

8. Of the three different Moving Averages, which one is more likely to give an investor a false signal?
   a. simple   b. exponential   c. weighted

9. Moving Averages are *commonly* used with which *one* of the three different indicators?
   a. Candlesticks   b. MoneyStream   c. price graph

10. Wise investors are ones who don't rely just on one technical indicator. They review other technical indicators, such as Support and Resistance Levels, Balance of Power, and Time Segmented Volume.
    a. true   b. false

Chapter 6 Quiz Answers

1. *False.* Moving Averages are calculated by taking the closing prices for a certain number of days and dividing the total number by that selected number of days.

2. As a longer-term investor, it's best to use a *long* Moving Average, which allows for less movement and a better long-term picture.

3. It's the *exponential* Moving Average that has more volatile swings because the calculated data is based more on the most current prices.

4. The terms "front-loaded" and "back-loaded" are used when calculating the data of *weighted* Moving Averages.

5. When either or both the Dow Jones Industrial and Nasdaq Composite drop below the *200-day* Moving Average, investors become alarmed that the market may be in a bearish cycle.

6. *True.* Moving Averages can be added to many other technical indicators, such as Volume, MoneyStream, Time Segmented Volume, and others.

7. *True.* Moving Averages can be recalculated as often as every minute by day traders. Longer-term position traders use daily, weekly, or monthly Moving Averages, which are calculated by their selected time frame.

8. Because the *exponential* Moving Average is calculated by using the most recent closing price of the investment, it tends to be more volatile and can give off false signals because of recent price movement of the stock/index.

9. A Moving Average can be used with Candlesticks, Money-Stream, and price graphs. *Price graphs* are more commonly used by investors, allowing them to see if their investment remains above the Moving Average as a bullish signal. When the price drops below the Moving Average, investors seek other technical information to see if the stock is becoming bearish.

10. *True.* Wise investors don't rely on only one technical indicator. It's best to always review several different technical indicators and parameters before reacting. The more research you do, the better you'll feel about the investment.

chapter 7

MoneyStream

MoneyStream is another wonderful technical indicator providing investors the opportunity for further research of individual stocks or indexes. It began as a personal indicator of the Worden Brothers. It is a proprietary indicator that aims to identify large systematic accumulation and distribution. Because it is proprietary, we don't know exactly how it's configured.

MoneyStream is buying or selling pressure as money is going into or out of a particular stock. Why is this important and how can it affect you as an investor? It's important because it can affect the direction the stock moves. An example would be a large investor who's looking to make a purchase of 10,000 shares of XYZ. The buyer knows that if she were to buy 10,000 shares all at one time, the stock value would increase, costing her more as the stock ran up. Systematically accumulating stock means that the buyer is accumulating the stock slowly over time without causing the price of the stock to rise dramatically.

The same would apply for systematic distribution. The seller has a large amount of stock to unload and doesn't want to alarm the market and cause the price to drop dramatically. Therefore, he sells the stock slowly over time while still trying to get the best price possible. The sales time frame can be daily, weekly, or even longer, depending on how much stock is to be sold. Systematic accumulation and distribution is known as hidden buying and selling. It reminds me of a teapot on the stove. At first it's quiet until it accumulates enough pressure; then it reacts by setting off a whistle. The same theory applies with the pressure of systematic accumulation and distribution. Once the large investment has been completed, the stock may continue its accumulation or distribution pressure, causing the stock to continue the same direction. How does viewing MoneyStream help investors? Simple; it allows them to see what's happening behind the scenes as these large investments are being made.

Generally when using MoneyStream you'd look for divergences. The automatic linear regression lines in both the price and indicator profiles can show important divergences at a glance. The chart is set up so that you can make direct comparisons between the slopes of the price regression lines and the indicator regression lines. When the cumulative money lines are sloping upward at greater angles than those of the price, the stock/index is bullish. And when the regression lines are sloping downward more than the price, it's bearish.

The stock rises in value when there's a lack of supply; when there's an overabundance of supply, the stock drops in value. With that in mind, would you want to be buying a stock as everyone is beginning to sell the same stock? No. Would you want to be selling the stock as investors begin to buy the stock? No. Well, there you go. MoneyStream gives you a better understanding as to whether there's more overall buying or selling. Its indicators are somewhat different than many other technical indicators because its formula is made up of both the price and the volume. MoneyStream can offer powerful benefits. To add it to your charts, you must first select the proper tab (1–12) you'd like the indicator added to. Then, press the X key on your keyboard to delete all other indicators. After you've deleted the old indicator, press Y on your keyboard to add MoneyStream. Figure 7.1 shows an example of this.

Select the middle as your preference for the chart insertion, then make your color choice. Yellow is commonly used when referring to the MoneyStream indicators. After you have completed these steps, you may elect to enlarge your chart by clicking on the box located in the upper right corner. Figure 7.2 indicates the price graph and MoneyStream with recession lines. Figure 7.3 shows a good example of a Moving Average being added to the MoneyStream as another indication of confirmation of either bullish or bearish signs.

figure 7.1   Biogen Inc. (BGEN)

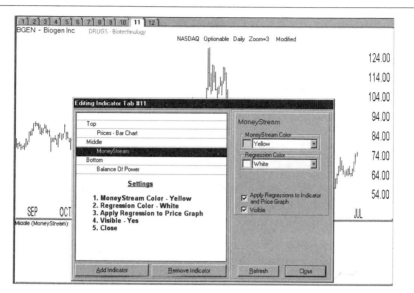

TC2000.com chart courtesy of Worden Brothers, Inc.

figure 7.2   Biogen Inc. (BGEN)

TC2000.com chart courtesy of Worden Brothers, Inc.

figure 7.3   JDS Uniphase Corp. (JDSU)

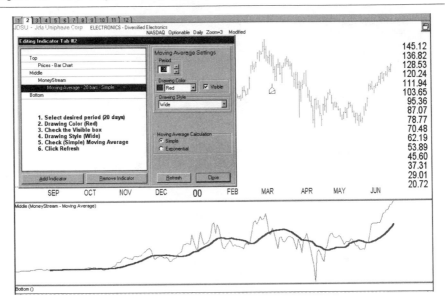

TC2000.com chart courtesy of Worden Brothers, Inc.

Chapter 7 Quiz

1. What is the purpose of the MoneyStream indicator?
   a. accumulation   b. distribution   c. both

2. The buying and selling pressure going in and out of a stock can affect the value.
   a. true   b. false

3. Investors who slowly accumulate stock are doing so in small amounts to avoid driving the stock price up suddenly, allowing them to slowly accumulate the stock at the lower prices.
   a. true   b. false

4. When an investor with a large amount of a stock to sell sells the stock in small increments to avoid driving the price down, he or she is using systematic distribution.
   a. true   b. false

5. Investors who understand accumulation and distribution have the advantage of knowing when to buy or sell.
   a. true   b. false

6. What other indicators can be helpful when added to MoneyStream?
   a. Balance of Power   b. Moving Averages   c. Volume Bars

7. MoneyStream indicators are different from many other indicators because they are comprised of what?
   a. volume   b. price   c. both

8. The easiest way to delete an indicator to add MoneyStream is by pressing what key on the keyboard?
   a. K   b. X   c. D

9. Now that you've deleted the old indicators, you can press which key on the keyboard to add the Moving Average indicator?
   a. T   b. A   c. Y

10. What color is commonly used when referring to MoneyStream indicators?
    a. green   b. cyan   c. yellow

Chapter 7 Quiz Answers

1. The MoneyStream indicator is used to help identify *both* accumulation (buying) and distribution (selling).

2. *True.* Price movement is affected by increased buying and selling of an individual stock. This is why MoneyStream adds value to an investment by allowing investors to identify the buying and selling pressure.

3. *True.* Accumulation is done in small amounts to avoid large increases in the stock value, as the buyer buys a large amount at lower prices.

4. *True.* Systematic distribution is when an investor sells a large amount of stock in small increments to avoid driving the price down with one large sale.

5. *True.* MoneyStream enables investors to see when large amounts of stock are being overbought and oversold.

6. *Balance of Power* and *Moving Averages* added to MoneyStream allow investors to follow both indicators at the same time with a better understanding of when to buy or sell an investment.

7. MoneyStream indicators are comprised of both a stock's *volume* and *price* movement.

8. To delete an indicator to add MoneyStream, you would press the *X* key on your keyboard.

9. After deleting an old indicator, you would press the *Y* key on your keyboard to add MoneyStream.

10. The most commonly used color for MoneyStream indicators is *yellow*.

chapter 8

Time Segmented Volume

Time Segmented Volume, more commonly referred to as TSV, is another proprietary technical indicator provided by Worden Brothers. I'm covering TSV now to give you a chance to compare it to the other indicators. I've found TSV to be the most rewarding technical indicator in my toolbox; it has become a great asset for my investment charting.

Figure 8.1 shows an example of an 18-period Time Segmented Volume.

Because Time Segmented Volume is a proprietary indicator, we don't know exactly how it is configured. We do know that it is calculated from a stock's price movement and volume movement. As the name suggests, TSV is a variation of different time segments of both the price and the volume. Variations of both the price movement and the volume movement are compared in order to uncover periods of accumulation (buying) and distribution (selling). By combining both the price and the volume movement of a stock, the TSV can alert us of a stock that may have a sustained price swing in one direction or another. This segmented direction swing is also commonly referred to as the change of a stock's character. Signs of a character change can indicate that the stock may be changing its price direction from bearish to bullish or from bullish to bearish.

The difference between TSV and other technical indicators such

figure 8.1   Vignette Corporation (VIGN)

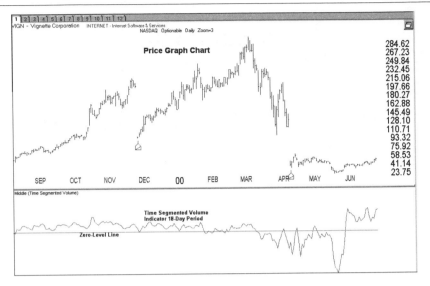

TC2000.com chart courtesy of Worden Brothers, Inc.

as Stochastics, Candlesticks, and Moving Averages is the *volume* portion of the indicator. Many other technical indicators are based solely on just the price movement of the stock. Price-related technical indicators can have a tendency to give more false buy or sell signals. TSV can help alert investors of false signals. A false signal occurs when a stock appears to be moving in one direction according to the price movement but the volume indicators show the stock volume moving in the opposite direction of the stock price. This occurs when a price moves up in value while the stock has more selling volume than buying volume. The opposite can occur as a stock price drops in value and the buying volume increases. This occurs most commonly due to activities of market makers and specialists.

A stock price can be controlled by several different sources. One of the largest sources of control is stock market makers and specialists. Because they make (control) a market between a buyer and seller, they also tend to control the price movement of the stock. Does this mean that they can or will run a stock up into the hemispheres or down to the ground? Not at all. They don't have that much effect because of their regulation by the Securities and Exchange Commission

(SEC). However, because they do have some control of individual stock prices, I'm going to explain one of the most common reasons why market makers/specialists will drive a price up or down for their benefit. Investors who utilize technical indicators with volume movement can see these actions occur and avoid false gapping signals.

The most common and misleading price movement of a stock is known as gapping. Gapping is when a stock begins trading (the next market day) at a higher or lower price than the previous day's closing price. Gapping commonly occurs because of pressure from investors to buy or sell a stock into the close of the market. Market makers and specialists take advantage of pressure selling and buying to generate a profit between the bid and ask price of the stock. Closing buy or sell pressure can put market makers/specialists in a position where they may have overbought or oversold a stock as the market closed for the day. The next morning what often occurs is the opposite of the previous close of the stock. If buyers at the close of the market bought the stock aggressively, the stock may then begin a sell-off at the open the next trading day. Figure 8.2 shows an example of an individual stock that gapped down upon the market opening. As the stock shows a decrease in its price value, in-

figure 8.2   Home Depot Inc. (HD)

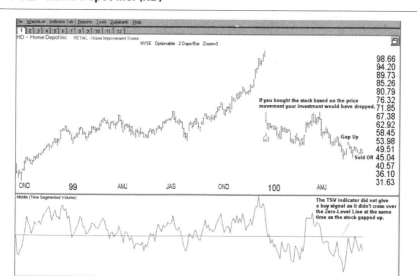

TC2000.com chart courtesy of Worden Brothers, Inc.

vestors tend to sell on a false indication thinking that the stock is going to continue dropping in value. As the selling continues to occur, market makers/specialists are now buying the stock at the lower price to cover their oversold position from the previous day. The same applies if the stock is being oversold into the close of the market. Figure 8.3 shows an example of an individual stock that gapped down on the opening of the day. Yet two days later the stock gapped and moved higher.

The market makers or specialists will gap the stock up to attract investors, again only to sell what they overbought previously. Gapping up or down of individual stocks is very common and can create a false movement of the stock because a change of direction can occur immediately, creating a loss to an investor. This is another reason to become better educated with technical indicators so you can identify these false movements by noticing the volume movement of the stock.

Now that you have a better understanding of TSV indicators, let's walk you through the steps to add TSV to your elected tab indicator (1–12). Right-click your mouse or the indicator tab (top left section screen), then highlight "Add Indicator" and "Time Segmented Volume," as seen in Figure 8.4. By doing so you should have brought up Figure 8.5,

figure 8.3   Dell Computer Corp. (DELL)

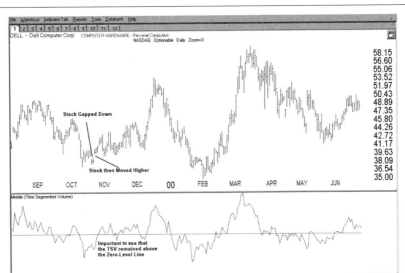

TC2000.com chart courtesy of Worden Brothers, Inc.

figure 8.4 Dell Computer Corp. (DELL)

TC2000.com chart courtesy of Worden Brothers, Inc.

figure 8.5 JDS Uniphase Corp. (JDSU)

TC2000.com chart courtesy of Worden Brothers, Inc.

asking you whether you are going to add the TSV to the top, middle, or bottom of your price chart. I prefer to add TSV to the middle. The next step is editing the TSV Time Period, Drawing Color, Visible, Drawing Style, and Moving Average Calculation. Review Figure 8.6 to see my selected settings for each of these five different choices. Investors commonly ask what TSV parameters they should use. However, the exact TSV parameters used are really somewhat arbitrary.

Many investors elect to use an 18-day period, yet it's common to view a chart with a 26- or 31-bar TSV. These parameters tend to change from investor to investor, depending on the investment time frame. The smaller the number, the more sensitive the indicator (which simply means the indicator will tend to be more responsive to price and volume fluctuations). Investors who elect to invest for a shorter time frame elect to use a shorter parameter, such as 18 days. By increasing the number or parameter of the TSV, you will effectively reduce the indicator's sensitivity, thereby filtering out the less significant price swings. If you elect to use a shorter parameter than 18 days, your TSV indicator will be more sensitive, creating larger swings

figure 8.6   JDS Uniphase Corp. (JDSU)

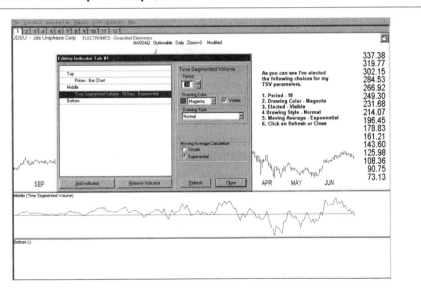

TC2000.com chart courtesy of Worden Brothers, Inc.

of movement. Longer-term investors still may elect to use an 18-day parameter and view the longer parameter by utilizing the computer keyboard numbers (1–9). By doing so with an 18-day parameter, you can change the time frame as you continue to press the higher keyboard numbers. Number 1 is normally a daily chart, but because we've elected an 18-day parameter, we're viewing the TSV for the last 18 days. By pressing the number 2 key on your keyboard, you're viewing the TSV on a 36-day parameter. As you continue to press the higher numbers, your parameters will increase. Remember: Each keyboard number represents one day, and that should be multiplied by 18 days because your TSV parameters are set for 18 days. In this example if we were to leave our TSV parameter at 18 days, each keyboard number would represent the following parameters as we multiply the keyboard's number by the elected 18-day parameter: 1 = 18 days; 2 = 36 days; 3 = 54 days; 4 = 72 days; 5 = 90 days; 6 = 108 days; 7 = 126 days; 8 = 144 days; 9 = 162 days.

Several technical indicators, such as TSV, use the terms "simple" and "exponential Moving Average calculation." Your preference again will center on your investment purpose and time frame. More conservative and longer-term investors prefer to use the simple indicator. A simple Moving Average indicator is an average that is equally weighted from the beginning to the end of its time frame. If you're using an 18-day parameter such as in the TSV example, all 18 days are equally calculated together to determine its simple Moving Average. Shorter-term investors who are looking for more of a recent effect of the Moving Average prefer to use exponential Moving Averages, which places more weight on the more recent data and not all 18 days. Simple and exponential Moving Averages can give the same effect as the 18-day TSV parameter. The simple Moving Average is more subtle, allowing for slower movement indications. The exponential Moving Average can be more sensitive, which can allow for more significant movements.

While the difference between a simple and exponential Moving Average is somewhat negligible when applied to TSV, I tend to set up my TSV configurations on an exponential Moving Average. The exponential Moving Average allows me to use a longer-term parameter, such as 31 days, yet I can still maintain a fair level of sensitivity in the indicator. As the market conditions change from bullish to bearish or bearish to bullish I will view the TSV with an 18-, 100-, and 200-day *simple*

Moving Average. This will be discussed further on in this chapter. Again, when setting your technical parameters, don't get caught up on what parameters are better than others. Your parameters should be based solely on two key points: your period of investment (short term or longer term) and the kind of return you are looking to receive.

Adding a Moving Average overlay on an existing TSV indicator can help you follow the stock movement and select a more desirable entry or exit point. I never look at a TSV indicator without calculating a Moving Average of the TSV, which I overlay onto the TSV indicator. There are a couple of reasons for this. First and foremost, I like to see where the Moving Average is in relation to the level line. Figure 8.7 shows an example of the Moving Average in conjunction to the level line. And, second, I like to see how TSV behaves relative to its Moving Average. For example, is TSV staying above or below its Moving Average for the measurable period of time and can its reaction be an indication of a change of character? Figure 8.8 shows a perfect example of a change of character. Nokia (NOK) was at $61 per share. As the TSV indicator crossed below the Moving Average, the stock began to drop

figure 8.7   JDS Uniphase Corp. (JDSU)

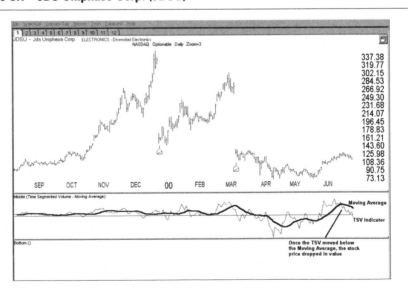

TC2000.com chart courtesy of Worden Brothers, Inc.

figure 8.8   Nokia Corp. Ads (NOK)

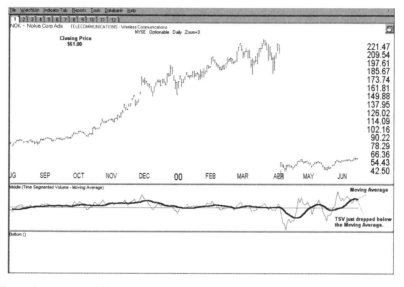

TC2000.com chart courtesy of Worden Brothers, Inc.

in value. You will also notice that once the TSV crossed below the level line, the stock continued to drop to $48.25 per share. Figure 8.9 shows that the drop in price occurred in only five trading days.

Now that you've reviewed both figures, let's explain how the TSV and its Moving Average are interpreted. There are really only three different things to consider when interpreting a TSV indicator pattern: positive/negative divergence, location of TSV, and movement of Moving Average with the TSV. The first two components are significantly more important than the last one. First, I prefer to see if a positive or negative divergence has formed between the stock price and the TSV indicator. For example, if the price has surpassed its previous peak and the corresponding TSV indicator has not, it constitutes a negative divergence between the stock price and the TSV indicator. Figure 8.10 shows an example of a negative divergence. The theory is that since the price peak is unconfirmed by the TSV indicator, it should eventually result in the price pulling back.

The second thing I take into consideration is the location of TSV

figure 8.9   Nokia Corp. Ads (NOK)

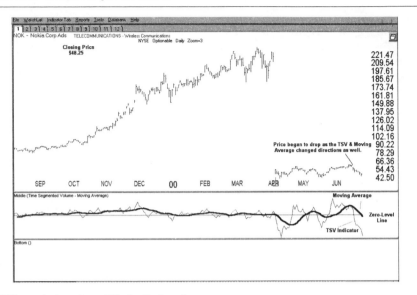

TC2000.com chart courtesy of Worden Brothers, Inc.

figure 8.10   Sun Microsystems Inc. (SUNW)

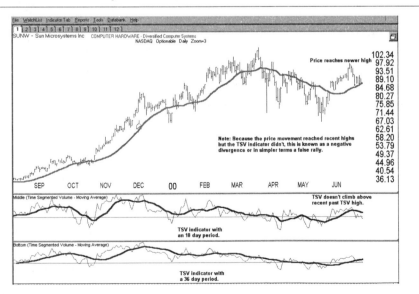

TC2000.com chart courtesy of Worden Brothers, Inc.

relative to the level line. A TSV that is above the level line is positive (see Figure 8.11); a TSV that is below the level line is negative (see Figure 8.12).

The third thing I look at is TSV's Moving Average relative to the level line. The same rules apply to the Moving Average as with the TSV indicator. Above the level line, as seen in Figure 8.13, usually signifies a positive (bullish) technical indication; below the level line, as seen in Figure 8.14, signifies a negative (bearish) technical indication.

When considering all of these factors, it is important to note how reliably TSV and Moving Average worked in the past on the same stock and/or within the context of a particular time frame. If the indicators haven't worked reliably in the past, it stands to reason that they might not work in the present. It is common for certain stocks to react differently with different technical indicators. You must remember that TSV calculations arise from both the stock's price movement and volume movement. These calculations change daily as the stock volume and price do. Sudden changes in either the volume or the price can affect the reaction of the indicators. If you've found that us-

figure 8.11   Vignette Corporation (VIGN)

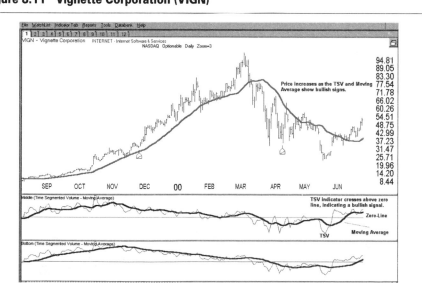

TC2000.com chart courtesy of Worden Brothers, Inc.

figure 8.12   Nokia Corp. Ads (NOK)

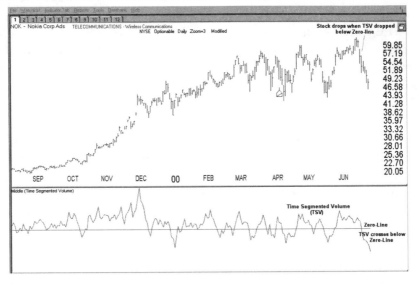

TC2000.com chart courtesy of Worden Brothers, Inc.

figure 8.13   Juniper Networks (JNPR)

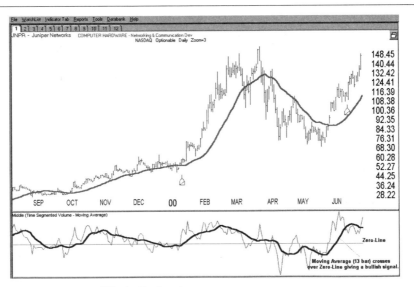

TC2000.com chart courtesy of Worden Brothers, Inc.

figure 8.14   Microsoft Corp. (MSFT)

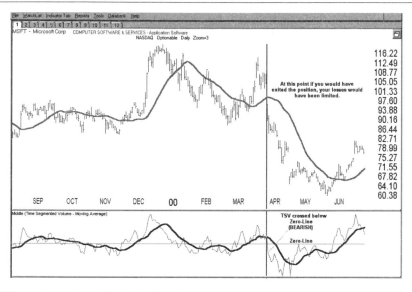

TC2000.com chart courtesy of Worden Brothers, Inc.

ing an 18-day TSV worked in the past but no longer is giving you accurate indications of the stock movement, consider changing to either a shorter or a longer time frame. A longer TSV time frame will smooth out the movement, allowing for less sudden swings; the shorter time frame will create more sudden swings.

While you may find Time Segmented Volume extremely beneficial by itself, always review the TSV with a Moving Average. To add the Moving Average to your TSV chart, first place your mouse arrow in the desired window (middle or bottom). Then right-click the mouse as seen in Figure 8.15, go to "Add Indicator," then "Moving Average," and left-click your mouse. You now have opened the "Add Moving Average To" window. Figure 8.16 shows this example; now select "Top," "Middle," or "Bottom" for location and left-click "OK." Now you have opened the Editing Indicator Tab, which will allow you to duplicate Figure 8.17 or set your own parameters for the Moving Average. Again, once you've selected your parameters, click on "refresh" and your selected Moving Average will be added into the same box as the TSV indicator.

Once again, you may elect to change your parameters with the

figure 8.15   Microsoft Corp. (MSFT)

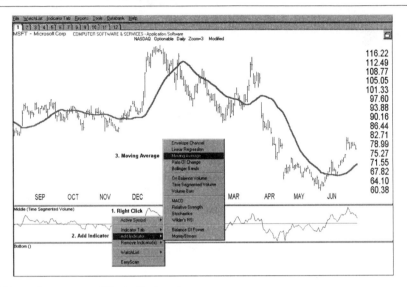

TC2000.com chart courtesy of Worden Brothers, Inc.

figure 8.16   Microsoft Corp. (MSFT)

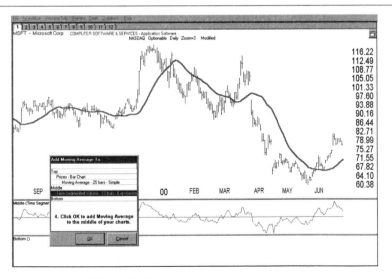

TC2000.com chart courtesy of Worden Brothers, Inc.

figure 8.17   Microsoft Corp. (MSFT)

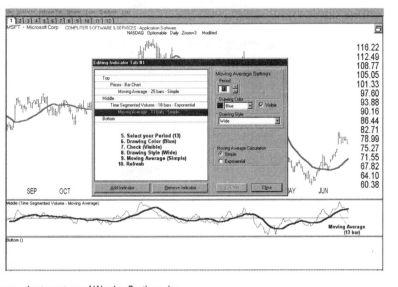

TC2000.com chart courtesy of Worden Brothers, Inc.

Moving Average such as you would with TSV if you're not able to see the proper buy or sell signs. TSV and Moving Average are like any other technical indicators and will not be right 100 percent of the time. The most important aspect of any technical indicator comes from the investor's ability to make changes when needed. Don't assume that once you've set your parameters, you won't need to change them.

Figure 8.18 is a complete TC2000 chart with my favorite indicators and their settings. The top portion of the price graph (Chart A) shows the stock's price movement with an overlapped 25-bar Moving Average. The middle indicators (Chart B) are my 18-day Time Segmented Volume and a 13-bar Moving Average. And the bottom indicators (Chart C) are a 36-bar TSV with a 21-bar Moving Average overlapped onto the TSV. Having both 18-bar and 36-bar TSVs on the same page enables me to see both a short- and long-term view of the stock's direction. These are the indicators that work best for me. Figure 8.19 shows the Nokia (NOK) stock dropping in value as seen by viewing the indicators. I've drawn a vertical line at the point when the

figure 8.18   Vignette Corporation (VIGN)

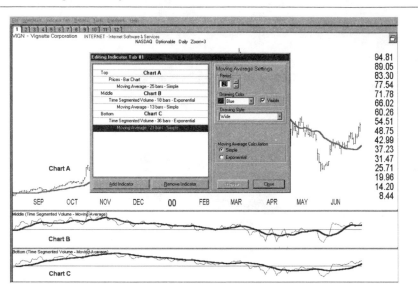

TC2000.com chart courtesy of Worden Brothers, Inc.

figure 8.19   Nokia Corp. Ads (NOK)

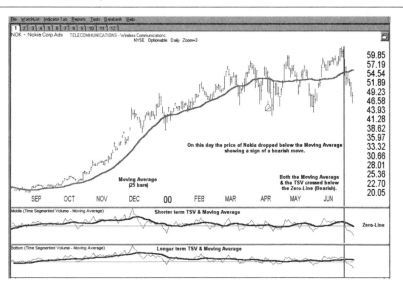

TC2000.com chart courtesy of Worden Brothers, Inc.

stock became bearish. The vertical line shows the price dropping below the 25-day Moving Average, and both the short- and long-term
TSV and Moving Average crossing below the level line.

Before we conclude this chapter on Time Segmented Volume (TSV)
I'd like you to view three more figures which can also help you determine a stock or index's next movement. What you're about to review
works well with both individual stocks as well as with indexes. Be sure
you take into consideration that indexes consist of several stocks and
more volatility, and when viewing the TSV of a single stock its calculation is based on an individual stock price and volume movement only.

Our first stock is Yahoo! (YHOO), Figure 8.20. As you can see, the
stock has had a great past for performing very well but it, like many
other stocks, was experiencing a time of correction. The first pattern
you're looking for when viewing this chart or any other chart is the
stock's Support and Resistance Levels. As you'll notice, I've taken the
time to draw in what I believe are the Support and Resistance Levels.
We may have a difference of opinion regarding the stock's Support and
Resistance Levels, and that's okay. What were looking for is a pattern

figure 8.20   Yahoo! Inc. (YHOO)

TC2000.com chart courtesy of Worden Brothers, Inc.

in which the stock trades sideways within a certain range between its Support and Resistance Level. As you'll notice in Figure 8.20, Yahoo! traded in a really tight pattern for several months, alerting us that it was going to break out to the upside or to the downside. If you look at the TSV indicator you'll notice that the TSV traded in a tight pattern also. The important indication you need to identify is that the price of the stock was trading in a certain pattern and the TSV was in a flat sideways pattern. The benefit of being able to identify these patterns is important if you're looking to get an idea of what will be the next move for the stock. In this example, Yahoo!'s next move was *down*. After you've been able to determine the support and resistance pattern for the price, you can easily identify that the TSV was remaining in a tight pattern close to its level line.

Your next major indication of the stock movement is the 200-day Moving Average. As you can see in Figure 8.20, Yahoo!'s trading range was below its 200-day Moving Average, and for several months the stock couldn't cross back above that 200-day Moving Average—a sure signal that the stock was more bearish than it was bullish. Yahoo!'s next move was definitely down, as the price of the stock dropped from $135 to $53.

Before you view the other examples, remember that the advantage of using the TSV indicator is because it's based on both the stock price movement and its volume. Another important key to note is that these patterns are best identified when using the 100- or 200-day Moving Average. I use the 100-day Moving Average as an alert to watch the stock closely. The 200-day Moving Average is the point in which I must make a decision (close out the long position, open a short position, or hedge my position) as it's a stock's strongest long-term Support Level. As you have heard and now have seen within this chapter, when stocks break below their 200-day Moving Average, the stock becomes extremely bearish and its bottom is very difficult to identify.

Figure 8.21 is Apple Computer (AAPL), selected to show you a bullish trading pattern. Yahoo! was trading in a sideways pattern as AAPL was in an upward pattern. What you should notice with both Figures 8.20 and 8.21 is the direction of the TSV indicator. During the elected time frame when the stocks were trading at or near their 200-day Moving Average, the TSV was flat. Viewing only the price chart of AAPL you could be misled into thinking the stock was going to continue upward, yet viewing the TSV indicator you should have been

figure 8.21   Apple Computer Inc. (AAPL)

TC2000.com chart courtesy of Worden Brothers, Inc.

alerted that it was flat. The final decision to exit the stock and/or take a short position was confirmed when the TSV indicator dropped below the level line. Four days later the stock gapped from $54 to $27 and continued to drop lower.

Figure 8.22 shows an example of Amazon (AMZN), as it formed its strongest Support Level below its 200-day Moving Average. The point I'd like to make about this example is similar to that of Figures 8.20 and 8.21, except that you'll notice that the stock broke below its 200-day Moving Average during January. Why is this such a concern? It's important to notice this because January was an extremely *bullish* market. As many stocks were increasing to higher highs, AMZN dropped below its crucial 200-day Moving Average. You'll also notice the stock crossed back above its 200-day Moving Average but could not remain there very long. The 200-day Moving Average, which is known for being the strongest Support Level, became a strong Resistance Level.

Now view Figure 8.23: You'll see I've identified the next crucial points of Amazon. A second Support Level was established, then a gap down below its second Support Level, the retesting of its previous

figure 8.22 Amazon.com Inc. (AMZN)

TC2000.com chart courtesy of Worden Brothers, Inc.

figure 8.23 Amazon.com Inc. (AMZN)

TC2000.com chart courtesy of Worden Brothers, Inc.

Support Level, and then a further drop in value. As you'll notice the TSV indicators, the bearish signal was given during the second Support Level, which was an indication that the stock was going lower.

Now that you've reviewed the different charts and benefits of Time Segmented Volume (TSV), I'd like to give you a few pointers. A flat TSV can be an indication to watch the stock closely as it soon may change directions. Be cautious of stocks that gap up or down because it could be only a short movement before a large directional movement. Finally, if you're unsure whether the stock is going to move lower, consider the TSV indicator as a reason to limit the downside, and use stop losses when needed.

Chapter 8 Quiz

1. Even though Time Segmented Volume is proprietary information of Worden Brothers, we do know that the calculation is comprised of both a stock's price and volume movement.
   a. true   b. false

2. What is an important level when viewing a TSV indicator?
   a. plus line   b. minus line   c. level line

3. A TSV indicator cannot be added to other technical indicators.
   a. true   b. false

4. When viewing a TSV indicator with an 18-day rather than a 36-day time frame, the movement of the indicator can tend to be _____?
   a. slower   b. same   c. faster

5. When using a TSV indicator and viewing a daily price chart, it's best to look for a _____ divergence if you're a bullish investor.
   a. positive   b. negative

6. When utilizing a TSV indicator, it may also be very helpful if you were to add which one of the following indicators?
   a. Stochastics   b. MoneyStream   c. Moving Average

7. A TSV indicator can be helpful with both short-term and long-term investments; however, it is more beneficial when used longer term.
   a. true   b. false

8. Because TSV indicators consider both the stock's price and its volume movement, it's safe to say that when the price is down, the stock will trade lower.
   a. true   b. false

9. When setting your TSV criteria, it's common to use an 18-day time period for shorter reactions. Many have found the ___-day

TSV period to work best for a more conservative movement on a longer time frame.

a. 21   b. 25   c. 30

10. When using a Moving Average that is overlaid onto a TSV indicator, it is best to follow both indicators and allow both to cross above the zero line if you are bullish and to cross below the zero line if you are bearish.

a. true   b. false

Chapter 8 Quiz Answers

1. *True*. Time Segmented Volume indicators are composed of both the stock/index price and its volume. Many investors have found that indicators that utilize both the price and volume movement are more advantageous in volatile market conditions.

2. When viewing a TSV indicator, the *level line* is the point at which the next movement of the stock may be bullish or bearish. Investors react when the TSV indicator crosses above or below the level line.

3. *False*. TSV indicators can be used along with other technical indicators. The most common indicator used with TSV is an 18- or 25-day Moving Average.

4. An 18-day TSV indicator shortens the time frame of the data used to calculate the movement of the stock and creates a more volatile and *faster*-moving indicator.

5. Identifying a *positive* divergence is a bullish sign as the TSV indicator shows higher highs as the price graph shows lower lows.

6. Adding a *Moving Average* to a TSV indicator can help confirm a true change of character. Wait for both the TSV and the Moving Average to cross above the level line, as this indicates a change of directions from bearish to bullish.

7. *False*. TSV indicators can be used with both short- and long-term investments by changing the parameters to meet your investment needs.

8. *False*. Just because the price is trading lower doesn't indicate that the stock will continue to drop. Understanding technical indicators gives investors the ability to identify an entry or exit that isn't based solely on price movement.

9. Ideal TSV time frames are 18 days for shorter viewing and *25* days when viewing longer time frames. Again, all investors

are different and so are their investment purposes. Other parameters may work as well or better for you.

10. *True*. When using both a TSV and a Moving Average, it's best to follow both indicators and allow them to cross over the zero line as a bullish signal and below the zero line as a bearish signal.

chapter 9

additional indicators

This chapter provides a brief introduction of some of the other commonly used technical indicators, such as Candlesticks, Stochastics, MACDs, Bollinger Bands, and Volume Bars. It's important that investors realize that technical indicators are only as good as the investors who are using them. The indicators discussed here may prove very helpful to you. As an investor you'll study and implement many different indicators with different parameters; that's okay, as long as the end result is rewarding.

Candlesticks

Candlesticks are one of the most popular and oldest indicators still being utilized. Candlesticks were created in Japan to graphically represent the movement of the rice market. Then they were used for the futures market. It wasn't until later that investors began to see a value when using Candlesticks with the stock market. Candlesticks are used with bar charts. Many investors have found Candlesticks to be simpler to understand the daily movement of a stock.

The two main parts of a Candlestick are the body and the shadows. The body represents the daily movement of the stock, and the shadow indicates whether the stock closed higher or lower than the last trading day. A body's height is determined by its daily trading range. The top indicates its highest trading point of the day, and the bottom of the body indicates its lowest range of the day. A body that is filled in (black) indicates that the stock closed lower today than its previous close. When the body is hollow, the stock has closed higher that day than its previous trading day.

Shadows are thin lines that can be found on most Candlestick bodies. They can be seen on both the top and the bottom or only on one side of the body. The thin lines are known as shadows, and they represent the high and low prices that were reached during that trading day. Japanese refer to the upper line (shadow) as the hair and the lower line (shadow) as the tail. With the body, these shadows give the appearance of a candle and its wick. Candlesticks give investors the ability to see the trading range of the stock for each day. Figure 9.1 shows an example of a Candlestick chart with its body and shadow. Yet the daily movement isn't as important as the *pattern* of a stock's movement. Figure 9.2 shows examples of bullish and bearish patterns. Like other technical indicators, Candlestick charting will not give you a buy

figure 9.1 Cisco Systems Inc. (CSCO)

TC2000.com chart courtesy of Worden Brothers, Inc.

figure 9.2 Yahoo! Inc. (YHOO)

TC2000.com chart courtesy of Worden Brothers, Inc.

or sell signal. Various trading terms are used with Candlesticks, including Doji, Spinning Tops, Paper Umbrella, Stars, Gravestone Doji, Dragon Fly, Hammer, Hanging Man, and Shooting Star.

A basic Doji is nothing other than a stock that traded up and down during the day, yet it closed at or about the same price at which it began trading. Dojis are easy to identify because they have no body.

A Gravestone Doji is similar to the Doji, as it also has no body. However, the Gravestone Doji, as seen in Figure 9.3, has a long hair (upper line) indicating that the stock traded higher during market hours yet it failed to hold its upward momentum and closed back at or near its open price. To many this is a bearish sign.

Dragon Fly Doji, as seen in Figure 9.4, is just the opposite of a Gravestone Doji. It traded lower on the day, as seen by its tail, yet it closed at or near its open price. Simply put, the stock opened for trading and traded downward and by the close of the market it closed back at its opening price. This can be a bullish sign.

Two identifiable reversal patterns come to mind, the Hammer and the Hanging Man. The Hammer, as seen in Figure 9.5, is identified

figure 9.3   LTC Properties Inc. (LTC)

TC2000.com chart courtesy of Worden Brothers, Inc.

figure 9.4   Realnetworks Inc. (RNWK)

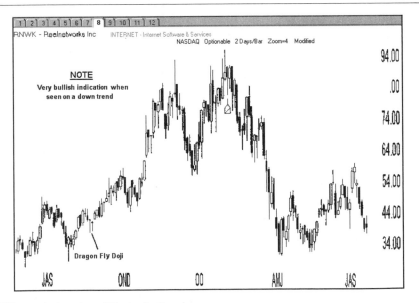

TC2000.com chart courtesy of Worden Brothers, Inc.

figure 9.5   Nextel Communications A (NXTL)

TC2000.com chart courtesy of Worden Brothers, Inc.

in a downtrend. (Its name comes from the fact that it's hammering out the bottom of a trend.) The Hammer is used to identify the turnaround in the trend as the stock opened lower and continued down but was able to retrace its direction to close up on the day. More consideration is given if the stock begins trading higher the next morning. When this occurs it can be a bullish signal.

Figure 9.6 shows an example of a Hanging Man, which was so named because the small body and long tail looks like a man hanging. Hanging Man can be identified in bullish uptrends, yet it is an indication of a possible sell-off. In order for a Hanging Man to appear, the stock price must trade much lower on the day but rally back up to close at or near its high. Unless the stock trades lower at the open the next day, you may be seeing a false signal.

Moving Average convergence divergence

Gerald Appel created Moving Average Convergence Divergence (MACD) for the purpose of producing specific trading signals. The primary rea-

figure 9.6   Adelphia Communication A (ADLAC)

TC2000.com chart courtesy of Worden Brothers, Inc.

son for its popularity among technicians is the fact that it is a very easy indicator to interpret. MACD indicators are very similar to price Moving Averages except they consist of three exponential price Moving Averages instead of just one or two simple price Moving Averages.

MACD can be displayed as two separate lines in the indicator window at the bottom of the chart. The first line plotted is actually the difference between two separate exponential Moving Averages. The first Moving Average should be set to a shorter-term time frame (e.g., 12 day) and the second Moving Average is typically set to a number about twice as long as the first. These parameters are determined by the user, based on his or her particular time horizons. The second indicator line is simply an exponential Moving Average of the first line. A common parameter used here is a nine-day Moving Average, but many traders experiment by varying the parameters since no indicator parameter works best for all market conditions.

MACD can be set up two different ways. The first is known as the histogram format, and the second is plotted with two lines. Histogram format looks similar to a Balance of Power format—positive increases above the level line and negative decreases below the level line. When using MACDs in a histogram format identify the "Rollover" movement from below the level line to above the level line as bullish and above to below the level line as bearish. Figure 9.7 shows both a bearish and bullish rollover of a plotted histogram MACD.

Trading signals with plotted line MACDs are produced when the solid line crosses through the dotted line. If it crosses up through the line, it's a buy signal. Conversely, if it crosses down through the line, it's a sell signal. (See Figure 9.8.) Many investors have found that positive and negative divergences between the MACD indicators and price are also highly significant and generally work well for picking major turning points. Figure 9.9 shows an example of my elected parameters for MACD. I use MACDs with Attain.com's real-time quote system as an entry or exit point on a two-minute chart. This chart allows me to see the most current movement in the stock, allowing me to get a better idea of where to set my sell or buy price. If the MACD is crossing upward with large accumulation, I'll set a higher price to sell. And if I'm

figure 9.7   America Online Inc. (AOL)

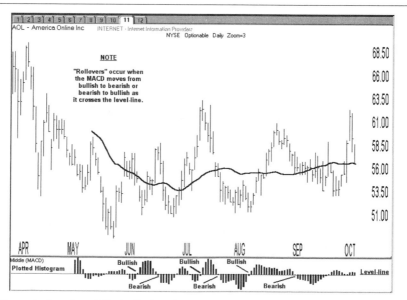

TC2000.com chart courtesy of Worden Brothers, Inc.

figure 9.8　America Online Inc. (AOL)

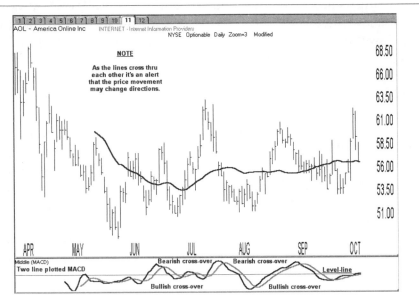

TC2000.com chart courtesy of Worden Brothers, Inc.

figure 9.9　Nvidia Corporation (NVDA)

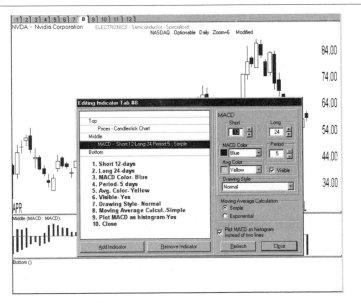

TC2000.com chart courtesy of Worden Brothers, Inc.

buying, I wait for it to cross lower with more accumulation. Again, all investors have their own patterns and preferences for charting.

Bollinger bands

Bollinger bands, developed and introduced by John Bollinger, are trading bands based on the volatility of prices around a simple Moving Average. When using volatility to compute the spacing between bands above and below the average, the spacing varies with volatility. Volatility in this case is measured as the statistical standard deviation computed on the same set of data as the Moving Average. To compute his bands, Bollinger recommends using a 20-day Moving Average, which is the arithmetical average of the previous 20 days of data. Volatility for the same 20 days is the variation of the data around the average for the last 20 days. Figure 9.10 shows the selected parameters. This variation is measured by the standard deviation of the data from the average. The actual trading band is plotted some number of standard deviations above and below the average. Aside from the

figure 9.10   Nvidia Corporation (NVDA)

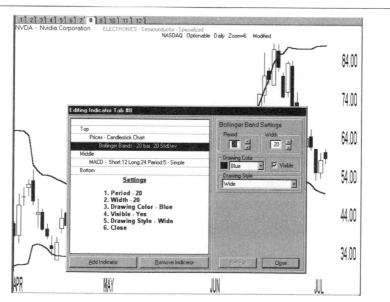

TC2000.com chart courtesy of Worden Brothers, Inc.

computational differences, Bollinger bands are used in the same way as other trading bands. In addition, Bollinger has developed several rules for these bands that can be used to look for indications of possible price moves.

Three Bollinger Rules

1. Sharp moves in price tend to occur after the bands tighten, and the closer to the average the better. Since reduced volatility denotes a period of consolidation, the first increase in the volatility after a consolidation tends to mark the start of the next move. Figure 9.11 shows the bands tightening.

2. Moving outside the bands signals a consolidation of the move until the price drops below or inside of the bands. Figure 9.12 shows an outside movement of the bands.

3. Moves starting at one band tend to go to the opposite band. Figure 9.13 shows the price chart moving from one band to another band.

---

figure 9.11   Oracle Corporation (ORCL)

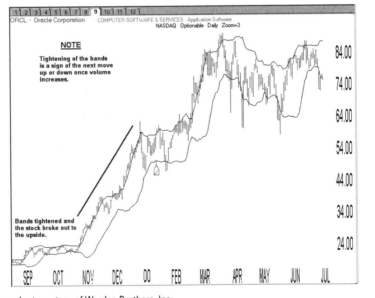

TC2000.com chart courtesy of Worden Brothers, Inc.

figure 9.12   International Business Machines (IBM)

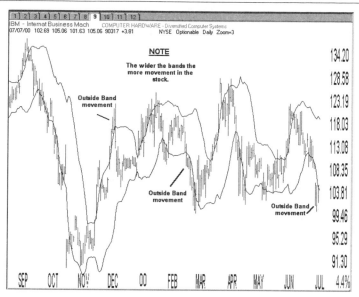

TC2000.com chart courtesy of Worden Brothers, Inc.

figure 9.13   Apple Computer Inc. (AAPL)

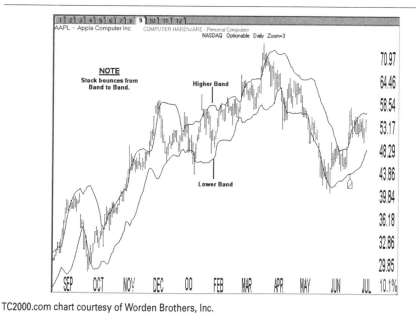

TC2000.com chart courtesy of Worden Brothers, Inc.

Stochastics

George C. Lane developed Stochastics, an indicator that measures the price velocity of a particular stock or market index. It essentially shows us where price is trading within a given range. The boundaries of the range would be the high and the low for a specific time period determined by the user. A Stochastic of 100 percent would mean price is currently trading at the extreme high of the range; and a Stochastic of 0 percent would mean price is trading at the extreme low.

Stochastics, like Relative Strength Index, help us determine whether the stock is overbought or oversold. When the Stochastics cross up through the 80 percent line, the stock is considered overbought. When the Stochastics are below the 20 percent line, the stock is considered to be oversold. The shorter the Stochastics period, the more signals the indicator will produce. However, if your period setting is too short, the majority of your signals will be false. A Moving Average of the Stochastics provides a basic buy and sell signal. When an overbought Stochastic turns down through its Moving Average, a sell signal is produced. When an oversold Stochastic moves up through its Moving Average, a buy signal is produced. Stochastics offer traders the ability to adjust the parameters to meet their own needs.

Commonly used parameters are 14, seven, and nine. Figure 9.14 shows you how to properly adjust the parameters for your needs. As for the drawing colors, the industry tends to use green as the positive indicator and red as the negative indicator. When both the green and red are at or below the 20 percent line, and the green crosses through the red, you have a bullish signal. The reverse is when the green and red are at or above the 80 percent line, and the red crosses through the green, you have a bearish signal. Figures 9.15 and 9.16 provide examples of bullish and bearish crossovers.

Envelope Channels

The construction of Envelope Channels is similar to that of price Moving Averages. In fact, an Envelope Channel is simply two lines formed around an invisible Moving Average. One line is above the Moving Average and one line is below it. The distance between the channel lines and the invisible Moving Average is a percentage deviation deter-

figure 9.14   Microsoft Corp. (MSFT)

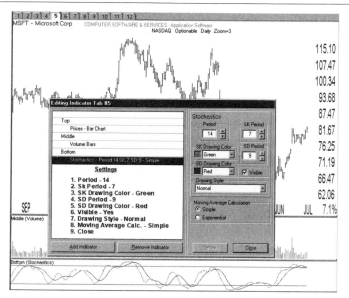

TC2000.com chart courtesy of Worden Brothers, Inc.

figure 9.15   Microsoft Corp. (MSFT)

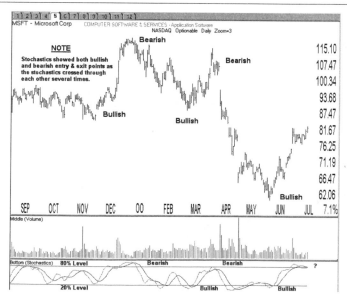

TC2000.com chart courtesy of Worden Brothers, Inc.

figure 9.16   Davox Corp. (DAVX)

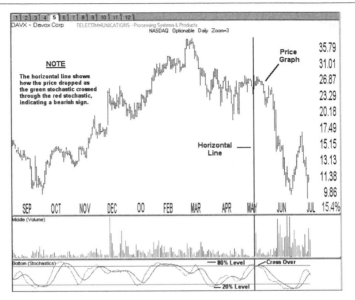

TC2000.com chart courtesy of Worden Brothers, Inc.

figure 9.17   Apple Computer Inc. (AAPL)

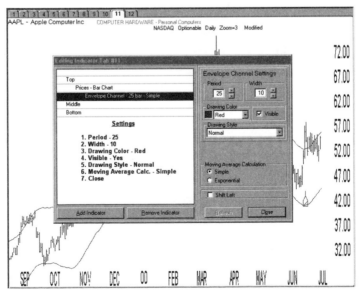

TC2000.com chart courtesy of Worden Brothers, Inc.

figure 9.18   Commerce One Inc. (CMRC)

TC2000.com chart courtesy of Worden Brothers, Inc.

mined by the user. This is referred to as the channel width. These channels help you see whether a stock is high or low within its price trend. Figure 9.17 indicates some Envelope Channel settings.

Volume Bars

Volume Bars are very similar to Candlesticks in that they allow you to see if the stock closed higher or lower than the previous close. Green bars identify positive closes, indicating that the closing price is higher than the close of the previous bar. Red bars show lower closes, indicating that the closing price is lower than the previous close. Figure 9.18 shows an example of Volume Bars.

Chapter 9 Quiz

1. How many technical indicators should investors view before making a final decision?
    a. one   b. two   c. several

2. What are the two main parts of a Candlestick indicator?
    a. tail   b. body   c. shadow

3. When viewing a Candlestick chart, the bullish Candlestick will be _____ and the bearish Candlestick will be _____.
    a. shaded   b. hollow

4. MACD indicators are simply explained as one line that crosses through another line giving a trade signal or plotted histograms which rollover from bearish to bullish or bullish to bearish.
    a. true   b. false

5. Bollinger Bands have a pattern of trading in tight or loose patterns, with the tighter the pattern the sharper the move in price.
    a. true   b. false

6. The main purpose of Stochastics is to assist investors in identifying whether a stock is overbought or oversold.
    a. true   b. false

7. Stochastics operate off two different levels, the bottom being the ____ percent level and the top being the ____ percent level.
    a. 20   b. 50   c. 80

8. What two colors are commonly used for Stochastics?
    a. red   b. yellow   c. green

9. When using Envelope Channels, an investor has the ability to see if the stock/index is higher or lower within the price trend.
    a. true   b. false

10. Volume bars enable you to see if the stock closed higher or lower than last week.
    a. true   b. false

Chapter 9 Quiz Answers

1. Always view *several* different technical indicators prior to making a trade.

2. The two main parts of a Candlestick are the *body* and *shadow*.

3. When viewing Candlesticks you'll see that the bullish Candlesticks are *hollow* and the bearish Candlesticks are *shaded*.

4. *True.* MACD consists of two lines: the solid line crossing through the dotted line, producing a trading signal, and a histogram, which rolls from above and below, the level line.

5. *True.* Bollinger Bands do trade in both tight and loose patterns. The looser the pattern, the larger the price fluctuation. The tighter the pattern, the smaller the price movement.

6. *True.* Stochastic indicators are used to assist investors to identify when stocks are overbought or oversold.

7. Stochastics operate off two levels, the bottom being the *20 percent* (oversold) level and the top being the *80 percent* (overbought) level.

8. The two most common colors used for Stochastics are *green* and *red.* As the green crosses the red, it's bullish; when the red crosses the green, it's bearish.

9. *True.* Envelope Channels are used to identify when prices are trading higher or lower within the channel.

10. *False.* Volume bars enable investors to see the price change of the previous day's close. Green indicates higher and red indicates lower.

chapter 10

technical corrections

Throughout this chapter I will discuss how to use technical indicators to identify and avoid major corrections prior to their occurrence. To do so, you as the reader must clear your mind of any and all other information that applies to the old school theory of buy and hold. You must not be brainwashed to believe that the only way to invest is to buy an investment and hold onto the investment long-term. Without going into detail and starting name-calling or finger-pointing, I will again publicly go on record by saying that the buy and hold theory is *not* what others are doing. What I'm saying is that brokerage houses, fund managers, and wise investors always know when and how to hedge their bullish investments to avoid large losses (limit their bullish losses with bearish investments) or take their profits prior to a correction and patiently wait before reentering the trade.

I'm an investor looking for both bullish and bearish opportunities. Once I've identified an opportunity to take profits, I will do so. I put a lot of emphasis on buying stocks on weakness and selling stocks on strength (bullish), as well as selling stocks on strength and then buying the stock back on weakness (bearish). It's important for investors to understand that money is made in all market conditions and directions. The toughest part of investing is determining when is the best time to buy or, more importantly, when is the ideal time to sell an investment.

As we review the many different technical indicators and price patterns shown in this chapter you'll realize that there is no such thing as the perfect entry or exit point. However, you will learn how to limit your losses and receive better returns when viewing selected indicators and price patterns. I say "selected indicators" only to alert you that I've found that some indicators that work well in bullish markets don't work as well in bearish markets unless you are paying close attention to the stock's price pattern, too.

For the first time in many years investors experienced a bear market correction during the year 2000. The unfortunate aspect of this was that a very large number of investors didn't know how to react to a bear market or they were limited by their investment firm and didn't have account approval to profit from such bearish corrections. It's important to always be sure that your investment account is approved for both shorting stock and buying put options. Again putting my neck out, I'll tell you that if your account cannot be approved for shorting stock and option investing, you're doing business with the wrong people and/or you need more education.

Is this information hindsight? Not at all. As the old saying goes, there are only two things that are guaranteed in life. One is *taxes* and the other is *death*. Well, let's add a third: We will experience another bearish stock market correction, the only question being when. Will it be today, tomorrow, next month, next year, or within several years? The answer is, you don't need to know or care, as long as you understand how and when to protect your profits and/or hedge your portfolio with bearish investments.

As a technical investor my greatest reward from a bearish correction is not the amount of profits that can be made, but the ability to share this information and charts with my readers so that the next time the stock market experiences a bearish correction investors will have a greater understanding of how to protect their investments and make money in a downward bearish market. Again at this time I'm going to remind you that I'm all for long-term investments as long as the investments are protected with an insurance program. This doesn't mean that you can call your local insurance agent and buy insurance on your portfolio. (Not a bad thought for a future business opportunity.) It's unfortunate that we can buy insurance to protect such assets on our home, auto, business, and family but not our investment portfolio. The only way to protect your portfolio is to know what strategies to implement and when to do so. As I mentioned earlier, the two most common ways of protecting a bullish portfolio is by hedging your investments by shorting stocks, selling naked put options, writing covered calls, or buying put options on individual stocks and/or the market indexes.

Identifying a bearish stock or market movement is done only when viewing technical indicators in conjunction with the actual price movement of the selected stock or indexes. As a visual example, view the price chart of Figure 10.1, which shows a simple explanation of why and when a bearish correction was about to take place within the Nasdaq Composite Index. As you can see I was focusing on only two simple indicators at this time, its Resistance Level at about 4,200 and its 200-day simple Moving Average. Taking both of these indicators into account I began changing my bullish outlook on the Nasdaq to a bearish outlook. Again I was changing my investment strategies and beginning to consider hedging my long-term investments.

I wanted to compare the bearish chart of the Nasdaq Composite, so I looked at the Nasdaq 100 (QQQ) also. Figure 10.2 shows that the

figure 10.1 Nasdaq Composite Index (COMPQX)

TC2000.com chart courtesy of Worden Brothers, Inc.

figure 10.2   Nasdaq 100 Tr Series I (QQQ)

TC2000.com chart courtesy of Worden Brothers, Inc.

QQQ tested its Resistance Level, then moved downward, and shortly after, it too dropped below its 200-day simple Moving Average.

After viewing each chart separately I wanted to compare the Relative Strength of the Nasdaq Composite Index (COMPQX) to the Nasdaq 100 (QQQ). As you can see with Figure 10.3, the Nasdaq 100 moves up and down somewhat the same as the Nasdaq Composite. By overlapping the two charts you're able to confirm that the 100 stocks of the Nasdaq 100 (QQQ) were reacting the same as those within the entire Nasdaq Composite Index. By utilizing the technical tool of Relative Strength, we're able to compare the thousands of stocks that trade on Nasdaq Composite Index with the selected group of 100 Nasdaq stocks which make up the Nasdaq 100 (QQQ). Instead of viewing just the COMPQX and assuming that it was truly a bearish correction, we took a few more minutes to confirm that not only were thousands of stocks moving downward but so were the selected 100 stocks of QQQ. Again, it's best to confirm your research to assure yourself that you're not reacting too fast.

Now that you've reviewed Figures 10.1, 10.2, and 10.3, look at Figures 10.4, 10.5, and 10.6 showing both the technical points of the price

figure 10.3 Nasdaq Composite Index (COMPQX)

TC2000.com chart courtesy of Worden Brothers, Inc.

figure 10.4 Nasdaq Composite Index (COMPQX)

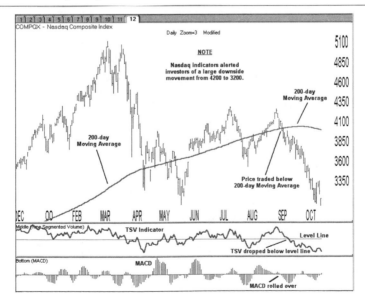

TC2000.com chart courtesy of Worden Brothers, Inc.

figure 10.5 Nasdaq 100 Tr Series I (QQQ)

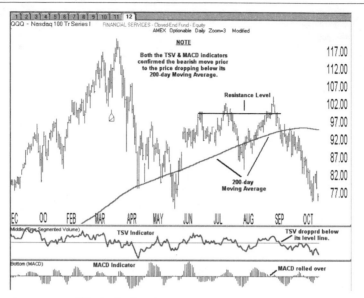

TC2000.com chart courtesy of Worden Brothers, Inc.

figure 10.6 Nasdaq 100 Tr Series I (QQQ)

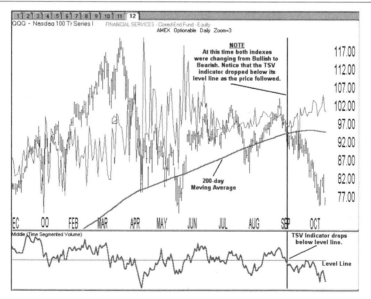

TC2000.com chart courtesy of Worden Brothers, Inc.

movement (resistance and 200-day Moving Average) combined with the technical indicators of the price movement and volume. Figures 10.4, 10.5, and 10.6 show both Time Segmented Volume and MACD indicators for the Nasdaq Composite Index (COMPQX), Nasdaq 100 (QQQ), and both of them combined. As you will notice by viewing these indicators with the price chart, the indexes truly were showing signs of a bearish correction. Both the TSV and the MACD indicator confirmed that the COMPQX and QQQ indexes were going to drop lower.

Okay, so you're still a long-term bullish investor and want to review more charts and technical indicators before selling your investments for a profit or hedging your long-term portfolio to limit your losses during a bearish correction. Allow me to show you the third index that is viewed highly as an indication of what direction the stock market may move. After being able to identify the bearish reversal with the Nasdaq Composite Index (COMPQX) and the Nasdaq 100 (QQQ), we're now going to view the movement of the Standard & Poor's 100 index, otherwise known as the OEX. Figure 10.7 shows both the Resistance Level and the 200-day simple Moving Average. Again, as

figure 10.7 Standard & Poor's 100 (OEX)

TC2000.com chart courtesy of Worden Brothers, Inc.

with all other technical charts, the picture doesn't lie. You now can see how all three indexes (COMPQX, QQQ, and OEX) were giving a warning signal alerting investors that the market was looking to make a change from the well-known bullish cycle to an unfamiliar bearish cycle. Figures 10.8 and 10.9 show additional confirmation of the bearish correction within the Standard & Poor's 100 index. Reviewing all nine different charts and indicators was more than enough to make a believer out of me. It was time to take off my bullish hat and put on my bearish hat. We were about to experience an all-around bearish stock market correction within the Nasdaq Composite Index.

Now that we've reviewed the Nasdaq Composite Index and smaller indexes within the Nasdaq Composite, let's look at the Dow Jones Industrial Average (DJIA), also known as the Dow 30 (DJ-30), to see if technical charting could alert investors of a bearish correction within that index. Many investors consider the DJ-30 a less volatile grouping of stocks compared to the Nasdaq Industrial. The 30 stocks that make up the Dow Jones are also known as blue chip stocks because they are nationally known stocks that have a long record of

figure 10.8   Standard & Poor's 100 (OEX)

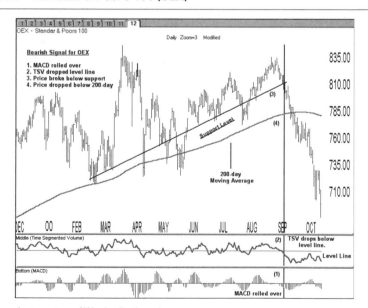

TC2000.com chart courtesy of Worden Brothers, Inc.

figure 10.9   Standard & Poor's 100 (OEX)

TC2000.com chart courtesy of Worden Brothers, Inc.

profit growth and dividend payment, and a reputation for quality management, products, and services. But does this mean that the stock can't drop in value? Absolutely not! Any and all stocks can and—at some point in their life probably do—drop in value. The concern is how far the stock can drop, and, if so, how long it will take for the stock to rebound back to its previous price. These are great questions to ask yourself when viewing technical indicators.

Let's now review Figure 10.10 and look at the DJ-30's short-term Resistance Level, Support Level, and 200-day simple Moving Average. Going back to January 14, 2000, the Dow reach a new all-time high of 11,750, but then it began a bearish correction as it dropped down to a low of 9,731 on March 8, 2000. A bearish correction of 2,019 points in only 52 days is a large correction within such an index, which has only 30 stocks. I'm bringing this to your attention so that you understand that sometimes stocks or indexes move up or down so fast that it's difficult to rely on just a support or Resistance Level, yet we can identify a change of direction by viewing other technical indicators.

Figure 10.11 shows the DJ-30 with 200-day Moving Average, sup-

figure 10.10 Dow Jones Industrials (DJ-30)

TC2000.com chart courtesy of Worden Brothers, Inc.

figure 10.11 Dow Jones Industrials (DJ-30)

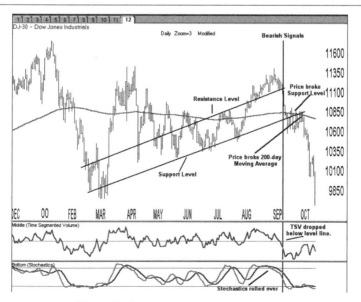

TC2000.com chart courtesy of Worden Brothers, Inc.

port and Resistance Levels, Stochastics, and an 18-day TSV indicator. After reviewing both Figure 10.10 and then Figure 10.11 you would have a better idea for what direction the Dow was heading.

Now, just as we did with the Nasdaq Composite, let's review the Standard & Poor's 500 Index (S&P 500), which has less volatility than the Nasdaq Composite and moves more like the DJ-30. Figure 10.12 shows a chart of the S&P 500, and as you'll notice the S&P 500 tested its 200-day simple Moving Average several times and finally broke down through it. When comparing two or even more charts to each other, remember that it's the 200-day Moving Average that is known as an index/stock's strongest Support Level. Many times I'll review indexes and stocks with a shorter Moving Average. I've found shorter Moving Averages to be more favorable when the market has large movements and volume. As we cover individual stocks and patterns I'll show you examples of several different charts utilizing different time frames for Moving Averages.

Knowing what you've read so far, I hope that you'll agree with me and see how rewarding technical indicators are. We've reviewed several

figure 10.12   Standard & Poor's 500 (S&P 500)

TC2000.com chart courtesy of Worden Brothers, Inc.

different indexes and how the price movement and technical indicators can keep us alert to the market direction; now let's move on and show you how to identify bearish individual stock movements. Let's focus on big-name stocks such as MSFT, HD, INTC, AAPL, T, LU, WCOM, YHOO, and DELL and review the stocks individually to see whether we can identify not only a change of direction but an exit point as well if you were long the stock.

Figure 10.13 is a chart pattern of MSFT. As you review the price pattern, the first thing you want to look at is the downward gap from the price of $106 to $90. Is it good news or bad news when a stock drops in value? It's definitely bad news! The worse the news, the worse its effect can be—not only on the recent price of the stock but also on the future growth of the stock as well. To keep things simple, I don't focus on the news; I focus on the effect the news has on the technical indicators. As you can see with Figure 10.13, MSFT gapped down two more times after the first drop of $16. What's important about this chart is that the stock dropped below its 200-day simple Moving Average. Once this occurred the stock continued to drop even more. How

figure 10.13   Microsoft Corp. (MSFT)

TC2000.com chart courtesy of Worden Brothers, Inc.

should an investor react to these technical indicators? After reviewing Figures 10.14 and 10.15, there was only one way to invest in MSFT, downwards. If you were a bullish investor long the stock or options, you should have closed out your position and sat on the sidelines. However, if you had the ability to short the stock or buy put options, you'd be in business to make some serious money as the stock continued to fall.

A very important fact that I'd like to point out about MSFT and any other stock that gaps down: If the overall market sentiment is bearish (which was explained earlier by viewing the individual indexes) and stocks gap down, it is a good sign that the stock may continue to drop lower, or the stock will just trade sideways for a very long time. Why is this important? Because too many investors think that just because a stock has a large drop in value it's a good time to buy the stock. This is not true; remember to review all your technical indicators and let the technical indicators tell you when to buy the stock.

Again, as MSFT continued to drop in value, I would not care to be the owner of the stock even when it was at $50 per share. It's important

figure 10.14   Microsoft Corp. (MSFT)

TC2000.com chart courtesy of Worden Brothers, Inc.

figure 10.15   Microsoft Corp. (MSFT)

TC2000.com chart courtesy of Worden Brothers, Inc.

to remember that we must keep our money working for us at all times, so we don't have to work for our money. I'm a strong believer in Bill Gates and MSFT, and once I see strong technical indications giving me a signal to go long the stock (buy call options or the stock), then and only then will I buy the stock or sell naked put options. As MSFT tests its lowest price in years and begins a bullish breakaway, I would consider selling naked put options (Chapter 12) with the intent to own the stock and/or receive a monthly premium. Referring back to Chapter 3, remember that as MSFT begins a bullish upward movement it will test new Resistance Levels which it must break through. Once this occurs and the Resistance Levels become a strong Support Level, you're looking at a good entry point. For example, MSFT is trading at $51 as it has tested the $50 Support Level; its Resistance Level will now be $60, meaning that it must break above $60 and not drop below it. If it does so, $60 is now its new Support Level. However, if it doesn't break through $60, it can return back down to its $50 Support Level.

As important as technical charting is, it's also very important to change your technical indicator time frames to view stocks/indexes during bullish or bearish breakouts. The two indicators which I change regularly are Moving Average and Time Segmented Volume, during a strong bullish run when I'm long the stock and after a stock such as the nine listed earlier have had a large (bearish) price correction. With a bullish move I will review the stock's Moving Average with a 30- and 100-day time frame to protect my profits. By changing my indicator time frames, I'm able to protect the profits and exit the trade at or near its 30-day Moving Average. If you don't, the stock may soon break below its 30-day Moving Average, then the 100-day Moving Average, and before long it's testing the 200-day Moving Average and you've given back some or all of your profits.

entry point

After stocks suffer bearish corrections, it's best to analyze the stocks with a 30-day Moving Average (along with other technicals) to determine an entry point of when to buy the stock or call options. To give you a better understanding of this, Figure 10.16 shows a 30-day Moving Average,

figure 10.16   Microsoft Corp. (MSFT)

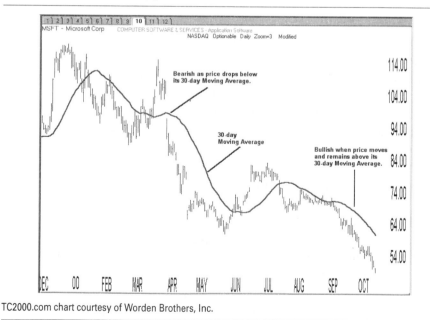

TC2000.com chart courtesy of Worden Brothers, Inc.

Figure 10.17 shows a 100-day Moving Average, and Figure 10.18 shows a 200-day Moving Average. What you should be noticing in the three charts is the distance between the current stock price and the three different Moving Averages. As investors we all know how important timing is, and if your viewing only the longer-term Moving Averages you could leave a lot of profits on the table if you don't enter the trade until after the stock moves above its 200-day Moving Average.

Once a stock has moved above its 30-day Moving Average it's time to look closely at other technical indicators and plan an entry point to buy the stock. As an example, compare MSFT's 30-day Moving Average (Figure 10.16) to its 100-day Moving Average (Figure 10.17); it's a difference of $18. Now go back and compare the 30-day Moving Average to MSFT's 200-day Moving Average (Figure 10.18); there's a difference of about $33 between the two Moving Averages.

As we continue on and look at the other eight listed stocks, remember two very important rules about the entry point. First, the stock must create a trading pattern above the 30-day Moving Average; secondly, such technical indicators as Stochastics, Time Segmented Volume, and MACDs must also be indicating that the stock is in a bullish upward movement. You must view these indicators to be sure that the stock is increasing in price as the volume increases; if not, you'll be looking at a false signal and the stock may drop back below its 30-day Moving Average and test its recent lows.

For sake of argument, as we view HD and the other seven remaining stocks I'm not going to say much about the bearish correction that occurred on April 12, 13, and 14, 2000. What I will bring to your attention is the fact that within these three days the Dow Jones Industrial Average dropped a total of 829 points—the largest three-day drop ever. Only two things can be said about such a correction: We will experience another correction again, and secondly, when we do, remember that the writing is on the wall giving investors an indication of what to expect. What occurred during those three days set an example of the next several/many months. During the months following that correction, the nine selected stocks we're discussing and many others performed poorly. The following months many stocks within both the Nasdaq and the Dow Jones suffered larger losses as they reported lower than expected earnings and/or revenues.

With this said, let's move on and look at Home Depot (HD). Known for its retail home improvement stores, HD is listed as one of the 30

figure 10.17   Microsoft Corp. (MSFT)

TC2000.com chart courtesy of Worden Brothers, Inc.

figure 10.18   Microsoft Corp. (MSFT)

TC2000.com chart courtesy of Worden Brothers, Inc.

Dow Jones Industrial Average stocks and trades on major exchanges such as the New York Stock Exchange and Pacific Exchange. It's important to know what exchange the stock trades on so we can compare the individual stock to similar and less volatile indexes such as the Dow Jones, S&P 100, or S&P 500. Our first comparison, Figure 10.19, shows the Support Level at about $53 and a Resistance Level at about $55, with a 200-day Moving Average. As you view this chart you should notice the most obvious bearish signal. Once HD dropped below its 200-day Moving Average, the stock tried to move back above that level but quickly dropped back down below the 200-day Moving Average.

Figure 10.20 shows the price chart of the Dow Jones Industrial Average (DJ-30). If you compare Figure 10.19 to Figure 10.20 you'll notice that Home Depot and the Dow Jones Industrial Average both were below their 200-day Moving Average at the time. Again the point I'm expressing here is that the Dow Jones was performing weakly as was Home Depot, a stock of the Dow Jones Industrial Average.

Now look at Figure 10.21, as we view Home Depot, with a 100-day Moving Average, Stochastics (14, 7, and 9 parameters), and Time Seg-

figure 10.19   Home Depot Inc. (HD)

TC2000.com chart courtesy of Worden Brothers, Inc.

figure 10.20   Dow Jones Industrials (DJ-30)

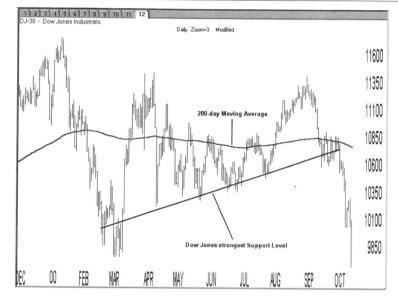

TC2000.com chart courtesy of Worden Brothers, Inc.

figure 10.21   Home Depot Inc. (HD)

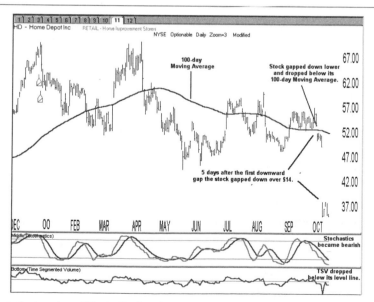

TC2000.com chart courtesy of Worden Brothers, Inc.

mented Volume (18-day). Using the 100-day Moving Average, you'll identify when Home Depot dropped below its 100-day Moving Average, the Stochastics crossed over, and the TSV dropped below the level line. Four days after the bearish signals and the first gap down, the stock gapped down another $14 from $49 to $35. After Home Depot gapped down the first time, dropped below its 200-day Moving Average, Stochastics crossed over, and the Time Segmented Volume indicator dropped below its level line, you should have closed out your long positions and considered going short. When considering reentering the stock, implement the same rules as those explained earlier.

Intel Corporation (INTC), a Nasdaq-listed stock, is in the semi-conductor-broad line business. More importantly, INTC is a leader in the computer chip business and is referred to often as an indication of what to expect of the overall computer industry. Review Figure 10.22, and locate the first downward gap during the beginning of September, the second downward gap during the middle of the month, and the final gap down at the end of the month. The pictures tell the truth and don't lie. As a photo of your children is worth thousands of words, a picture of the stock market is worth thousands of dollars. INTC's picture was about as ugly as a picture can get. The chart identified the bearish correction early and allowed investors plenty of time to exit the trade before it became even uglier as time passed.

Figures 10.23 and 10.24 show 100-day and 30-day Moving Averages. What is noticeably different between Figure 10.22 and both 10.23 and 10.24 is the point at which the stock price dropped below its averages. As you'll see, sometimes it may be best to use the shorter Moving Averages such as those seen in Figures 10.23 and 10.24. INTC has had such a large upside run within the last five years that it has split its stock four times within the five years. This positive growth has set the 200-day Moving Average so much lower than the price. In order for INTC to test its 200-day Moving Average it had to experience a serious reduction in its price.

With such stocks as INTC and others that have a past history of recent stock splits, it's normally best to view the short Moving Averages as seen in Figures 10.23 and 10.24. Shorter Moving Average allow for a closer tracking of the stock and can alert investors of problems sooner than a 200-day Moving Average. INTC's stock was trading at $57 when it crossed below its 200-day Moving Average. As with the 100-day

figure 10.22   Intel Corp. (INTC)

TC2000.com chart courtesy of Worden Brothers, Inc.

figure 10.23   Intel Corp. (INTC)

TC2000.com chart courtesy of Worden Brothers, Inc.

figure 10.24   Intel Corp. (INTC)

TC2000.com chart courtesy of Worden Brothers, Inc.

Moving Average, its price was $54, and viewing the 30-day Moving Average its price was $67.

Now that you've seen all three Moving Averages, look at Figure 10.25, which shows the technicals are indicating a bearish correction before the price drops below its 200-day simple Moving Average. As you'll notice, its strongest Support Level is higher than the 200-day Moving Average. Now look at Figure 10.26 as we use a 100-day Moving Average with an 18-day TSV. The vertical line shown in the figure indicates the point at which the stock changes from bullish to bearish. The difference between Figures 10.25 and 10.26 is not the technical indicators; as you'll notice, it's the difference between the 100-day and 200-day simple Moving Average. Your first concern with the stock is when it broke its 30-day Moving Average, and then its 100-day Moving Average. By following these indicators you should have exited the stock before its 200-day Moving Average and would have been able to limit your losses and avoid the third (largest) gap down.

I'd like to say that the perfect time to exit long positions is when a stock or index drops below its 30-day Moving Average. But because we don't live in a perfect world, the next best exit point would have been

figure 10.25   Intel Corp. (INTC)

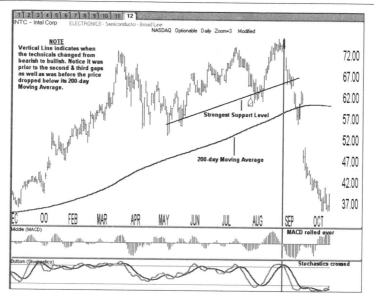

TC2000.com chart courtesy of Worden Brothers, Inc.

figure 10.26   Intel Corp. (INTC)

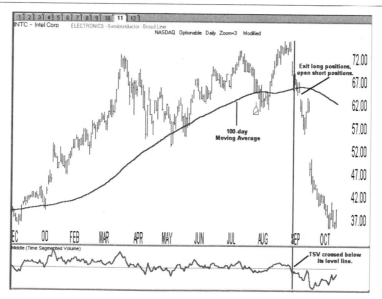

TC2000.com chart courtesy of Worden Brothers, Inc.

after the second gap down as the technical indicators confirmed the bearish correction.

Before I move on to our next stock, I'd like to bring up one point about INTC. During a presentation to a large group of investors, we viewed the same figures as shown here. After our evaluation of INTC's technical indicators, one lady spoke up and said, "Even though INTC's stock has dropped in value, it's still a good company and worth holding long-term." I responded by showing the group several other stocks that had recently dropped in value. Then I replied, "Sometimes it's best to identify a correction before it occurs and sell the stock knowing that you can always rebuy the same stock at a later date or move on to one that is moving in the right direction." My point was that regardless of what company experiences a large correction, it will take a long time and really positive news before the stock returns to its previous price. One last consideration: Always remember that once a stock experiences bad news, several other analysts will come out of the woods and also downgrade the stock, causing it to drop even further. As an investor who often invests in INTC, I use the wait-and-see approach before taking a long position in INTC. As the industry saying goes, INTC received quite the haircut as it dropped from $75 to $35 in only 45 days. On a brighter note, INTC has great upside potential.

Intel's charts were perfect examples of what to look for as an indication of when a stock changes from its bullish upward movement to a bearish downward movement. Now view the chart of Apple Computer (AAPL), shown in Figure 10.27, and identify whether the stock was in a bullish or bearish movement and at what price is its Support Level. As seen in Figure 10.28, AAPL reacted the same as INTC did when the MACD rolled over, the Stochastics crossed, then the stock tested its Moving Averages, as it then gapped down in price twice. You'll notice that the Moving Average in Figure 10.28 is 10 days instead of the more common 30, 100, and 200-day Moving Averages. Because both technical indicators turned bearish several days before the longer-term Moving Averages, it's best to shorten your Moving Average to about 10 days. This allows you to follow the movement closer as shorter time frames create sooner movements. Again, as I've repeated several times throughout this book, always shorten your indicators once you're able to identify a market correction forming. Allow yourself the opportunity to exit your long positions early to avoid giving back your profits or, more importantly, taking a big loss.

figure 10.27 Apple Computer Inc. (AAPL)

TC2000.com chart courtesy of Worden Brothers, Inc.

figure 10.28 Apple Computer Inc. (AAPL)

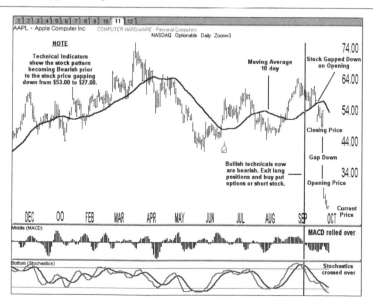

TC2000.com chart courtesy of Worden Brothers, Inc.

figure 10.29   AT&T Corp. (T)

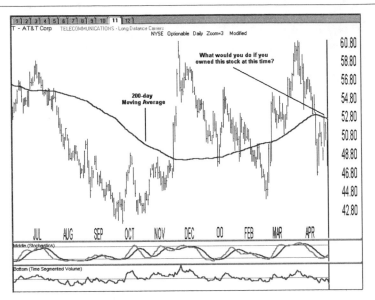

TC2000.com chart courtesy of Worden Brothers, Inc.

figure 10.30   Yahoo! Inc. (YHOO)

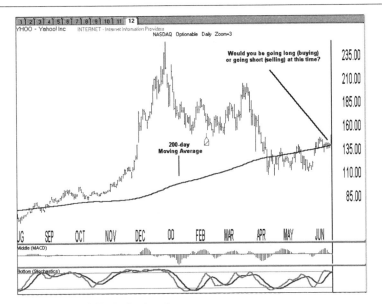

TC2000.com chart courtesy of Worden Brothers, Inc.

figure 10.31   Lucent Technologies Inc. (LU)

TC2000.com chart courtesy of Worden Brothers, Inc.

figure 10.32   AT&T Corp. (T)

TC2000.com chart courtesy of Worden Brothers, Inc.

figure 10.33   Yahoo! Inc. (YHOO)

TC2000.com chart courtesy of Worden Brothers, Inc.

figure 10.34   Lucent Technologies Inc. (LU)

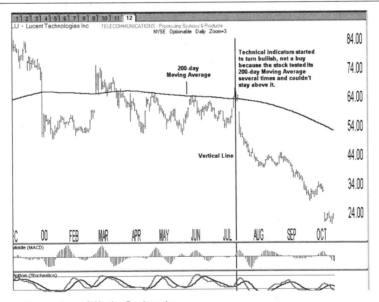

TC2000.com chart courtesy of Worden Brothers, Inc.

Take a look at Figures 10.29, 10.30, and 10.31. I want you to look at the last section of the chart where the vertical line is. Decide if you'd be opening long or short positions. Before you make these decisions take a pencil and draw your strongest Support Level on the price graph, then review the technical indicators located on the bottom of the chart. It's important to remember the rules about the 200-day Moving Average and its location relative to the current price. Before you read on, review those three charts and make a decision: Are you bullish or bearish? Now look at Figures 10.32, 10.33, and 10.34 and verify whether you made the right decision.

You should have been able to limit your losses if you were holding long positions. If you're an investor with the ability to take on short positions, you may have taken advantage of the bearish correction that occurred with AT&T, Yahoo!, and Lucent.

Chapter 11, "optional profits," can help you benefit from both call and put options.

chapter 11

optional profit$

To many people, a stock option is not only a foreign language but a scary phrase. Yet historically, option investing existed as early as the time of the Phoenicians. Option investing began prior to the stock market. The Phoenicians and the Romans used option contracts for the delivery of goods they transported on their ships. Then in the first half of the seventeenth century, option contracts were used in the Netherlands during the tulip craze.

Contracts were regularly traded for the option to buy or sell (known today as the *right*, not the obligation) a particular type of tulip bulb at a specific price (known today as a strike price) by some future date (known today as the expiration date). Tulip dealers could buy call options to ensure that they would have adequate supplies in case the price rose substantially. (Call options allowed dealers to buy a set amount of tulips at a predetermined set price before a certain date.) Tulip growers, on the other hand, could buy put options (allowing them to sell for a set price in case the tulip value dropped) to ensure they could sell their bulbs at a set price.

The past once again paved the road of the future. At 10:00 A.M. Eastern Standard Time on April 26, 1973, the investment world changed forever. That morning the Chicago Board Options Exchange (CBOE) began trading listed stock options in the smokers' lounge just off the main trading floor of the Chicago Board of Trade. Chicago Board Options Exchange cofounder and first president Joseph W. Sullivan stated that options were an opportunity of a lifetime and were long overdue. Prior to the existence of the CBOE, put-call dealers traded options in an over-the-counter market. Typically, dealers would advertise in each morning's edition of the *Wall Street Journal* a list of their put and/or call options. An investor wanting to buy or sell any of the advertised options would call the dealer.

Then the Investment Act of 1934 created the Securities and Exchange Commission, giving it the power to regulate trading options and allowing for their existence. Later the SEC allowed the trading of stock options at the CBOE. Prior to April 26, 1973, the CBOE was used to trade commodity futures. The Options Clearing Corporation (the OCC) was added to the option market next. The OCC was established to issue the options contracts and to guarantee clearance, settlement, and performance. Buyers could rely on the OCC to faithfully match and execute their option contracts. The OCC also made it possible for buyers or sellers to close their option positions in an open market with a party other than the dealer. Prior to the CBOE and the OCC, investors who bought and sold stock options had to go back to the put-call dealer to execute their options. Today options are traded not only on the CBOE but also on other exchanges, including the American Stock Exchange, the Philadelphia Stock Exchange, and the Pacific Stock Exchange.

fundamentals of options

Now that you have an understanding of where and when options began, it's time to understand exactly what you're investing in and the best way to invest. The most popular word that comes to mind when considering option investments is the word "risk." An investor's ability to fully understand options can limit the amount of risk involved. The main difference between investing in stocks and investing in stock options is that with an option, you can lose your entire investment. With a stock, the only way to lose the entire investment would be if the stock went to a value of $0.

With stocks, investors can always wait out the return of the stock value. As an educator, my goal is to educate investors, not to advise them on which investment or strategy is better than the next. However, I will state that I prefer always to invest in the option before owning the stock. Why? I'll explain in detail in Chapter 12. I have the knowledge it takes to invest in options, and by investing in options I have less risk. Let me repeat the second part of that statement: I have *less risk*. Option investing is different than stock investing. Option investors have to have more knowledge than investors who are brainwashed to buy and hold stock. Why do you think this is? Could it be because there's more opportunity for the brokerage firms? As stated in my book *Trade Stocks Online*, my investment purpose is simply to make money (taking my profits when I see fit). With this in mind, let's begin the explanation of option fundamentals.

options explained

An option is the right, not the obligation, to buy (known as a call) or sell (known as a put) an asset (stock) for a certain price (known as the strike price) on or before a certain date (known as the expiration). The key point of this definition is that the investor of the option has the right, not the obligation, to buy or sell the option within a certain time frame *and* if the investor doesn't exercise the right prior to the set time frame, the *total* investment will be worthless. Options get a bad name (risk) because investors allow their options to expire worthless and lose money simply because they didn't know what they were doing and/or didn't properly research their choice of investment and check the chart and technical indicators.

option contract

Options can be bought or sold only as a contract. Each contract represents 100 shares. The minimum purchase would be one contract for 100 shares; there is no set limit for the maximum. It always is best to buy or sell large numbers of contracts in increments of 20 contracts at a time. When doing so your odds of getting filled faster are much better, as option makers tend to delay or even change the bid and ask price to their benefit. Example: If you were to place an order to buy/sell 40 contracts, your order may take longer than if you placed two orders, one for 20 contracts and another for 20 contracts. You have generated two trades—20 contracts each; this may be two separate commissions but at least you executed the trade faster. Another nice advantage of using my direct execution system (www.attain.com) is that it allows me to buy/sell partial orders within five minutes for one commission. This is a great advantage when trading stock or options. When exercising your order to sell stock or have stock put to you due to an option position, remember that you can only buy or sell stock in increments of 100 shares.

call option

A call option can be both bought and sold, just like put options. To keep things simple, I will focus on buying call options during bullish upward markets. In Chapter 12 I explain another bullish option in detail with selling naked put options. I prefer to trade naked put options, then sell covered calls. (The only difference between covered and naked positions is simply that the word "covered" means you own the stock and "naked" means you don't.) Investors have many opportunities to invest in options, as option investments allow investors to implement such trades as bull call spreads, bear call spreads, bull put spreads, bear put spreads, covered calls, straddles, strangles, and others. I've always made it a point to use the KISS method of teaching option investing: Keep it simple, stupid. The stock and option investing is complicated already; why publish another advanced over-the-head financial book?

When buying call options, investors have the right to exercise their opportunity of buying the stock at a set price on or before a predetermined time. It's important to remember to buy call options only if you're investing for an upward movement. The two ways of investing in a stock with an upward movement would be to buy the stock or buy the call option. Buying the call option enables investors to spend less money and still realize a financial gain if the stock increases in value. Option investors have two choices: (1) Exercise their right and *buy* the stock any time before or on their selected expiration date for the predetermined price; or (2) *sell* the option and take the realized profits.

Options are overlooked, as many inventors don't realize that they have the right to sell their option for a profit or loss any time prior to its expiration. (This can be done within minutes, days, weeks, months, or even years.) When investors purchase a stock, they tend to invest for a longer period of time. With options, many investors invest just to obtain a profit or limit their losses and exit the position if the stock moves in a downward direction. Buying and selling of call options is a bullish investment.

put option

Put options are similar to call options, giving investors the right, not the obligation, to have the stock put to someone else or vice versa and give someone the right to put the stock to you. Many investors appreciate up-and-down volatility in a market because put options allow them a form of insurance. Put options will be explained in detail in Chapter 12. Put option investing can be either a bullish or bearish investment depending on investors' purposes. When investors sell put options, they want the market or selected stock to *increase* in value; when they buy put options, they want the market or stock to *decrease* in value. The word "put" means the right to force something upon someone. In this example it would be the stock. Bullish investors tend to buy put options during a bullish market to hedge their bullish investments in case of a market correction.

strike price

The "predetermined price" of an option is known as its strike price. Strike prices are set dollar amounts that buyers or sellers agree to buy and sell an investment for. These prices are set figures determined by the OCC and vary according to a stock's value. Strike prices consist of three different dollar amount increments, which are $2.50, $5, and $10. Stocks with a value of $5 up to the point of $25 trade in increments of $2.50. These increments are $5, $7.50, $10, $12.50, $15, $17.50, $20, and

$22.50. Stocks valued from $25 to $200 trade in increments of $5. These examples would be $25, $30, $35, $40, $45, $50, $55, $60, $65, $70, up to the dollar amount of $200. The final strike price increment is $10, which starts at $200 and increases such as $210, $220, $230, $240, $250, and as high as the stock price.

out of the money

If you're investing in options, it's important to know the terms "out of the money," "at the money," and "in the money." "Out of the money" means that you have selected an investment strike price that is higher than the current stock price. Example: You're considering an option on a stock that is trading at $51. Knowing that option strike prices are in increments of $5, at this point you look at the next highest strike price above the stock price of $51. It is $55. If the stock is trading at $51, this option investment would be considered "out of the money" because the strike price (right you have to exercise your option to buy the stock) is higher than the stock value of $51. This investment is out of the money by $4—the difference between the strike price of $55 and the stock price of $51. Because out-of-the-money options can be rewarding only with larger upward movements, the risk factor is higher yet the option price is less expensive. Less cost always equals more risk.

at the money

Option strike prices that are equal to the stock's current price are known as at-the-money options. Both the current stock value and your selected strike price are the same. Example: Stock is trading at $50 and you selected to buy or sell the $50 option. Then your option strike price is at the money. Rule of thumb is that the at-the-money options have a tendency to be less desirable than the out-of-the-money or in-the-money options. The reason appears to be because the option makers at this point don't know which direction the stock may move. At-the-money options don't have any intrinsic value (equity), meaning that the option premium consists only of time value. These at-the-money options are less expensive than in-the-money options, but they can be more of a risk.

in the money

Of the three different choices, more option investors tend to trade in-the-money options. A call option is known as being in the money when the selected strike price of the option is lower than the current stock price. Example: The selected strike price is $50 and the current stock price is $54. Your option has an intrinsic value (known as equity) of $4, which is the difference between the two prices of $54 and $50. In-the-money options are more expensive than both at-the-money and out-of-the-money options. However, in-the-money options have a better delta ratio.

When trading put options, the in-the-money, at-the-money, and out-of-the-money rule is the complete opposite. Example: Stock is trading at $53 and the selected strike price is $50. The put option is out of the money by $3. This is further explained in Chapter 12.

delta ratio

A delta ratio is a percentage in which an option will move in conjunction with each $1 movement of the stock. The larger the delta ratio, the larger the option price can increase in an upward movement. The same can be said for a decrease in the stock. The larger the decrease of the stock price, the larger the option can decrease. Bullish options have what is known as a positive delta (+.80), and put options have a negative delta (–.80). As an investor it's always best to make an educated investment that the stock has a good chance of increasing rather than decreasing. When buying call options, the higher the stock price travels, the higher the delta increases. The opposite occurs when buying put options. The farther the stock price drops, the higher the delta increases.

intrinsic value

When option investing, it's always good practice to compare different option strike prices to see which option offers the most rewarding intrinsic value. Intrinsic value is simply the equity in an option. To determine this you would subtract the difference between the option strike price and current value of the stock. The remaining value between the two prices is the intrinsic value (equity).

time value

The time value portion of an option is the amount of money that is paid (buying a call or put option) or received (selling a call or put option). This dollar figure consists of two parts; one is the amount of time the option consists of prior to its expiration date; the second can consist of what is known as fluff. This is a dollar amount that the market makers add or take away from an option based on their belief of how the stock will move. When buying a call option for a stock that shows great upward potential, market makers may inflate the premium. The reverse applies when buying a put option that may show a downward movement; market makers may inflate the premium as with call options.

expiration date

Expiration date is exactly that, a date at which time an option investment expires. As an investor you have the right to choose which expiration date you prefer. However, options roll out in a quarterly expiration cycle. Simply, you can always trade options for the current month (meaning that month of the current year), and options can be bought as far out as three years (known as LEAPS). The expiration date of your selected option is always the third Friday of the selected month you selected; however, the *technical* expiration is 12 noon on the Saturday following that third Friday. As public investors (non–exchange investors), we cannot trade options after the market closes on expiration Friday, so we must act by the close of the market on expiration Friday or sooner. The time difference between the close of Friday's market and Saturday noon following allows the Options Clearing Corporation to sort out all the exercised and expired options. Remember, when trading options, you as the investor have the right, not the obligation, to buy or sell on or before the expiration date (third Friday of your chosen month).

call option purchase

Currently I'm considering to buy a call option in the company Nokia (NOK), as the stock has recently completed a four-for-one stock split and is down $4\frac{9}{16}$ at $48\frac{7}{16}$. Dow Jones Industrial Average is currently down 187 points and the Nasdaq Composite is down 155 points as to-day's market trend is bearish. The first step to making an educated investment is determining the stock's recent Support Level, which in this example is $50, as shown in Figure 11.1. Nokia recently traded as high as $57 after the four-for-one stock split on April 11, 2000. It's obvious that the stock has great upside potential. The question is: How much and within what time? Being conservative, I wanted some time on my side, so I compared the June 50 call options to the July 50 call options. June $50 call options were trading at $2\frac{7}{8}$ bid × 3.00 on the ask side, and the July call options were trading at $4\frac{1}{2}$ bid × $4\frac{5}{8}$ on the ask side.

Because I use a real-time Level 2 screen provided by Attain.com, I can review the current option prices without calling a stock broker. This saves me time and gives me a chance to see what prices the other exchanges are offering. (Like stocks, options trade on different exchanges and can be offered at different prices.) I placed a limit order (set price at which I was willing to buy the op-

figure 11.1 Nokia Corp. Ads (NOK)

TC2000.com chart courtesy of Worden Brothers, Inc.

tion) for the day to buy 10 contracts (1,000 shares) of the Nokia July 50 call options. My limit price of $4\frac{1}{4}$ was a price that I selected between the bid and ask price. As the stock sold off a little more I was filled at the price of $4\frac{1}{4}$ for 10 contracts (1,000 shares). My investment was $4.25 \times 1,000$ shares (10 contracts) = \$4,250 + \$50 commissions totaling \$4,300. Trading options offers great opportunity when you know how to invest. One of the many positive opportunities is the ability to leverage your money. Think about it; I invested approximately \$4,300 to control 1,000 shares. The old-school way of investing would be to buy the stock, which would have cost me \$50,000 plus the commission.

My purpose was to trade the option for a profit and then sell within a short time and definitely before the option expired on the third Friday of July. As the owner of the July \$50 call option, I also had the right to buy the 1,000 shares of the stock on or before the expiration date of July. But I purchased these options as a corporate business investment (discussed in Chapter 13) so I'll be selling the options within a few days or weeks at the longest. It's now expiration Friday of May, and I have until expiration Friday of July, which gives me nine weeks for the stock to move upward. As I'm watching the stock now one and a half hours have passed and the stock has moved up from \$48 to \$50, which has increased the option I bought from $4\frac{1}{4}$ to $5\frac{1}{4}$.

If I were a day trader I would consider taking the \$1,000 profit; however, I'm a position trader looking for this stock to continue up in value within a certain amount of time to net me a greater profit. My decision to hold on to the call option was also because, as I mentioned, stocks have a tendency to find their strongest support and resistance levels at rounded numbers, such as the \$50 support price that Nokia is trading at now. Again refer to Figure 11.1 to see the strong Support Level at \$50. Because Nokia closed above this Support Level of \$50, I chose to hold the position until next week, at which time I will look for an exit point. Viewing Nokia's chart (Figure 11.2) I can see the Resistance Level at \$57. I will continue to use a trailing stop loss (a set price I choose that is just below the current bid price; if the stock starts trading downward, my sell order will automatically be filled, allowing me to protect my profits in case the stock continued to move down. Figure 11.3 (top) shows the actual buying confirmation of 10 contracts

figure 11.2 Nokia Corp. Ads (NOK)

TC2000.com chart courtesy of Worden Brothers, Inc.

at $4,250 and Figure 11.3 (bottom) shows the actual selling confirmation of 10 contracts at the price of $5,000.

Even though the resistance level for Nokia was $57, I elected to sell now as I was going to be out of town for a few days and the odds are the stock would drop back down to its support at $50. This move resulted in a profit of approximately $650, for nine trading days.

Figure 11.4 shows another great example of the chart, as the stock rose from $48⁷/₁₆ on May 19, just beyond $57 on June 5, an increase of $8.57 per share. As for the July $50 option, it rose from $4½ to $8½. The difference between the prices is $4 per share multiplied by 1,000 shares (10 contracts), to equal $4,000 profit for 11 trading days. Remember I sold my option early. If I were to hold the July option as originally planned I would have profited $4,000 for an 11-day trade instead of $650 for nine trading days. If I didn't elect to sell the option, I would be using a close trailing stop loss to ensure that if the stock doesn't remain above its resistance of $57 I've protected my profits in case the stock heads back down toward its Support Level of $50. Figure 11.5 shows an example why stop losses are important.

figure 11.3   trading confirmation slips

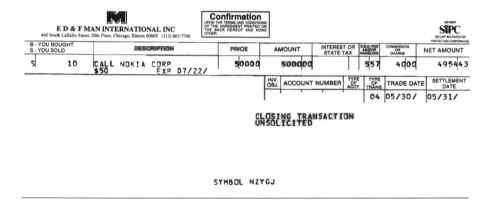

Nokia broke below its strongest Support Level and traded lower to approximately $35.

Sometimes when trading short-term options, it's best to take a profit if you are not able to follow the trade closely. Any profit is better than a loss. I'll wait for the stock to drop back down to its Support Level of $50 and then reconsider the trade, once the technical indicators look stronger. At that time I'll consider purchasing LEAPS (long-term equity anticipation securities) options. LEAPS can be written for as far out as two and a half years, which allows investors plenty of time for the stock to perform.

figure 11.4   Nokia Corp. Ads (NOK)

TC2000.com chart courtesy of Worden Brothers, Inc.

figure 11.5   Nokia Corp. Ads (NOK)

TC2000.com chart courtesy of Worden Brothers, Inc.

exercise your option

Remember, a call option is the right, not the obligation, to buy or sell an equity (stock) on or before a certain date (expiration date) for a certain price (strike price). If you bought a call option and the stock increased in value, you can elect to purchase the stock at the set strike price of your option. In order to do this, you must notify your broker that you currently hold the call option and would like to exercise your right. By exercising your right you have just taken the stock away from someone for that selected strike price. Using Nokia as an example, let's review what would happen. I originally bought 10 contracts (1,000 shares) of the July $50 call options for the price of $4.25 per share ($4,250). Let's say that the stock is trading at $57 per share, and you elect to buy the stock at the set $50 price. Your broker would execute the trade for 1,000 shares of Nokia at a price of $50 per share, costing you $50,000.

What is the benefit in doing this? The only benefit is if you like the stock and believe it has more upside growth, then you can benefit when you elect to sell the stock for the higher price. But if that was the case, then why didn't you just buy the stock instead of the option when the stock was trading at $48\frac{7}{16}$? Investors who buy call options do so for only two reasons: (1) to sell the option for a profit (I would rather get paid—sell a naked put option—to own a stock I like instead of paying for the right to own a stock), and (2) in anticipation of owning the stock after it has had a large bullish (upward) movement. The call option also allows investors a limited amount of risk if the stock takes a bearish (downward) fall.

When you purchase call options, your risk is only the premium you paid; with the stock, you can lose a lot more if the stock continued down. If you know what you're doing and how to analyze technical charts, call options offer the most powerful asset of all: leverage, the ability to utilize less money than if you were to buy the stock; yet in most winning situations option investing can offer greater returns than buying and holding stock. You be the judge as to what works best for you, but always remember to practice your trades first before spending your future. Most important, don't forget to implement stop loss orders when trading options. If the stock goes against you, be sure you know when and at what price to sell your option for a loss.

Never allow the market to take you out of the investment world. Control your losing trades just as you would your winning trades. A wise investor is one who admits he's made a mistake; a successful investor is one who acts upon his mistakes.

As an investor you will have trades that go against you. Know when enough is enough and how to stop the bleeding. Ninety percent of all options expire worthless because investors don't know what they're doing or they don't know when to limit their profits or losses. As I've always suggested, when trading options as a beginner, *always* buy yourself plenty of time and purchase options that expire in three or more months.

Chapter 11 Quiz

1. On April 26, 19__, option investing began in the smokers' lounge located at the Chicago Board Options Exchange.
   a. 70   b. 73   c. 75

2. The Options Clearing Corporation (OCC) was established to assure investors that all options were:
   a. issued   b. matched   c. exercised

3. Options are the right, not the obligation, to buy or sell for a certain price on or before a certain date. The certain date is known as the:
   a. execution   b. expiration   c. both

4. Option investments are done only in contracts, and each contract controls how many shares of the underlying stock?
   a. 50   b. 100   c. 200

5. As an investor who wanted to realize an upside movement on a stock, you would buy a put option.
   a. true   b. false

6. Options can be bought, sold, or exercised only in set prices known as "strike prices." The strike prices are in increments of $2.50, $5, and $10.
   a. true   b. false

7. An option investment which has more than six months of remaining time is known as a:
   a. long option   b. equity option   c. LEAPS

8. The term "intrinsic value" is referred to as the amount of equity in an option and can be figured by _____ your selected strike price from the current value of the stock.
   a. subtracting   b. multiplying   c. adding

9. All options like any investment have their share of risk however, options that are _____ the money can have the largest risk.

   a. in   b. at   c. out of

10. Option investing gives investors an opportunity to invest with less money and also benefit in both bullish and bearish markets.

   a. true   b. false

Chapter 11 Quiz Answers

1. On April 26, 1973, selected stock options began trading at the Chicago Board Options Exchange.

2. The Options Clearing Corporation was established to *issue* the option contracts and guarantee clearance, settlement, and performance.

3. All options have an *expiration* day, which is technically the third Saturday of each month; however, because the average investor cannot trade on Saturday, the expiration date is the third Friday of each month. It's important to remember that your options expire only on the third Friday of your selected month and year.

4. Option investments are traded only in increments of *100* shares equaling one contract. The smallest trade would be one contract (100 shares) and the largest trade is unlimited.

5. *False.* As an investor looking to invest in a bullish upward trend you would buy a call option. A call option gives the investor the right, not the obligation, to buy the stock at the selected strike price, or resell the call option when profitable.

6. *True.* Options can be bought, sold, or exercised only in set prices known as "strike prices." These set strike prices are determined by the value of the stock. Stocks trading between $5 and $25 trade only in increments of $2.50 ($5, $7.50, $10, $12.50, $15, $17.50, $20, and $22.50). Stocks that trade from $25 up to $200 trade in increments of $5, ($25, $30, $35, $40, $45, $50, and so on to $200). And finally all stocks of $200 and above trade in increments of $10 ($210, $220, $230, and up).

7. Option investments that have more than six months of time are known as Long-Term Equity Anticipation Securities (LEAPS®), and can be traded as far out as two and a half years from the current date.

8. When trading options you will hear the three important terms, in, at, and out of the money. An option is considered

to be trading in the money when the current stock price is trading above your selected strike price. The in-the-money portion of the option is calculated by *subtracting* the current stock price from your elected strike price. At-the-money options are when both the stock and the options strike price are the same, and out-of-the-money options are when the stock is trading below your selected strike price.

9. Options as well as any other investments have risk; when trading options that are *out of* the money the risk factor can greatly increase. The temptation of out-of-the-money options is the price. You'll find the price is less expensive because the risk is higher. Out-of-the-money options can have great value in a short-term time frame if the stock has a large movement or when trading LEAPS.

10. *True*. Option investing does allow an investor to use leverage as well as participate in a bearish market when buying put options.

chapter 12

put plays

Put investing by far can be the most rewarding investment known. However, again it's a strategy that requires complete knowledge and understanding. No one should sell naked puts or buy put options without properly evaluating the technical charts to gain a better indication of the stock's direction.

It surely is great when an investor has the ability to make money in a bullish (upward) market. But how about making money in a bearish (downward) market? Again, the largest asset investors have is their ability to react according to the market trend. As an investor I always found it rewarding when I could invest in a stock and make money regardless of its direction. As time has passed, the stock market has changed. Now technical analysis is required to determine proper entry or exit points of an investment. Before I cover the strategy of selling naked put options, it's my responsibility to explain the bearish opportunity for buying put options.

buying put options

Buying put options is the opposite of buying call options. Investors who buy call options are risking a certain amount of money in anticipation that the selected stock or index is bullish and will move up in value within a certain time. Investors buy put options when they are bearish with the intention of the selected stock or index dropping in value. Buying put options is similar to shorting a stock or index. Investors sell the stock at the higher price, then buy the stock back at a lower price, keeping the difference. Put options are no different except that they are a great deal cheaper than having to trade the stock. If you elect to buy put options, remember that the terms "in the money" and "out of the money" are the opposite of when buying call options.

Example: *Stock trading at $53*

Call Option	Strike Price	Put Option
Out of the money $7	$60	In the money $7
Out of the money $2	$55	In the money $2
In the money $3	$50	Out of the money $3

With call options, the option is in the money when the stock is trading above the selected strike price. With put options, the option is in the money when the stock is below the selected strike price of your option. To simplify things, when buying a call option, the profit is the difference between the right you have to buy the stock and at its current trading price. The higher the stock value increases, the higher the option premium increases. With put options, the profit is the difference between your selected strike price and the stock's current price. The lower the stock drops in value, the higher your option premium increases.

Remember, money can be made in all market directions. When buying call or put options, you have to be right because your investment is at risk. If the stock doesn't perform to your satisfaction, exit the position and limit your losses. The cardinal rule of investing is to always know why you invested and, win or lose, know when to exit. The rewarding part of selling naked puts is the fact that the stock's performance is what determines not only *at what price* to exit but *when* to exit the trade.

selling naked puts

Regardless of your trading experience or knowledge, selling naked put options is for any investor who's looking to make money, buy stock at a discounted price, or, most important, limit losses. These three advantages are exactly why selling put options is by far my favorite and most rewarding strategy. (Rewarding in the sense of making money as well as limiting losses.) Limiting your losses is even more rewarding than making a profit. Selling naked put options is the only investment strategy that allows so many opportunities with complete control and exits. Selling naked puts has two very important rules:

1. You must like the stock enough that you're willing to buy it.
2. You must agree to buy the stock for the selected strike price you chose.

Let me first start by explaining exactly what the words "selling naked puts" mean. "Selling" comes from the simple meaning that you're receiving money. When you sell a naked put you receive money. Because it's an option investment, the money is in your account the next trading day. "Naked" is a Wall Street term that means you are naked in the position and don't own anything. Basically you are selling someone the right to do something. "Put" means that you are giving someone the right/obligation to put a stock to you (force) you to buy the stock. Selling naked puts allows someone the right (not the obligation) to force a stock to you on or before a certain date (expiration date) for a certain price (strike price).

By this point you should be asking yourself why would anyone want to give someone the right to force the sale of his or her stock. Let me start by asking: Have you ever bought a stock and within 30 days it dropped in value and you lost money? Yes should be the correct answer, as we've all had this happen to us. Of course, some of you are saying no, because you think that just because you didn't sell the stock you haven't lost any money. In reality you have, because you could have bought the stock for less money, which would have given you more of a profit when you sold. Selling naked puts allowed me to make money during the bearish market correction in the middle of 2000 while losses took a large number of investors out of the market. I had always been such a bullish investor that I didn't see a need to sell naked puts. Once I started to see a change in the market's technical charts, however, I was able to change my investment strategy to sell naked put options. After spending a lot of time studying this strategy, I realized it had more benefits than any other stock market strategy. I must thank my investment mentors Mike and Stacy for their perseverance and time in helping me.

erosion of time

Option investing has two parts to the premium, equity and time. When buying call options, your premium erodes away each day, causing the time portion of your option to decrease in value. As long as the stock value increases, the call option will also; that is true. My point is that you paid for the time premium of the option and it erodes as time passes; the closer the option gets to its expiration date, the less the time premium. If the stock doesn't increase in value or even if it stays the same, the option will be worth a lot less—if anything—on expiration. As an investor I want you to change your way of thinking and open your mind to allowing time to work in your favor instead of against you. Remember, selling naked puts means "receive a premium," allowing you to take in the option's time premium instead of paying for it. When selling put options, we want the time to pass, causing the premium to decrease, which benefits us.

selected expiration

Past experience has proven that short-term put options are more rewarding than longer-term expirations. Investors often ask if it's best to sell the naked put two or three months out to retain the time premium into their account. My experience has been that it is best not to exceed the maximum of 30 days when selling naked puts. Example: Today is the third Friday of May, which is the expiration of May options. I'd be looking to sell naked puts today or Monday (the first trading day of the June options). My new expiration date would then be the third Friday of June. Later in this chapter I will show you why it's best to sell the shorter-term puts that allow you to roll out and down in strike prices if the stock drops dramatically in value. Doing so can limit losses if needed.

margin requirements

"Margin" is the amount of money that the brokerage firm requires to secure the investment. It's common with stock purchases that brokerage firms will lend a certain amount of money to investors and charge interest on the amount loaned. When purchasing stock, the industry margin tends to be 50 percent of the stock's total value. If an investor bought 1,000 shares of XYZ stock at a price of $40 per share, the total cost would be $40,000 if paid in full or $20,000 if the broker allowed the investor to buy on margin. As market conditions change, firms are known to increase the amount that investors must have in their accounts. This is very common with Internet stocks, which have huge volatility swings.

I've seen brokerage firms increase from the normal margin requirement of 50 percent to 80 percent, meaning investors must have 80 percent of the stock value in their account. The broker will lend only the remaining 20 percent of the stock's value. When this occurs, be aware that the broker may be preparing for a market correction or large reduction in a stock's value. Always be careful when borrowing money from your broker. It's not the additional commissions or interest rate that gets the best of investors, it's the broker's ability to close out investors' positions and/or accounts if the broker doesn't receive the funds in time to cover a margin call.

Margin requirements for selling naked puts are normally less than the 50 percent margin required when buying stock. In bullish markets brokerage firms often allow as little as 20 percent or 30 percent of the stock's value as margin. This brings up another example of money leverage. If we use the same example of 1,000 shares (10 contracts) at $40 per share, the cost would be $40,000 and the option margin would be 30 percent of the stock price equaling $12,000, and the option premium received for selling the put. If you were to buy 1,000 shares of the stock using the 50 percent margin, your cost would be $20,000. Let's assume we received an option premium of $3 per share × 1,000 shares (10 contracts) equaling $3,000. Your total margin for this naked put trade would be the 30 percent ($12,000) and the premium ($3,000) you received when you first sold the naked put. Example: $12,000 + $3,000 = $15,000.

Always remember that the margin requirement for naked puts changes daily as the stock price changes. If the stock increases in value, the 30 percent margin *increases* as the option premium received *decreases* in value. When the stock drops in value, the 30 percent margin *decreases* in value as the option premium *increases*. The Securities and Exchange Commission sets these margin requirements, but the margin requirement of different brokerages may vary. A common example of this is when the overall market trends change from bullish (upward) to bearish (downward). It's common to see brokerage firms increase the margin from as low as 20 percent to over 50 percent of the stock value. The .com companies that have negative earnings and don't have a record of making money are the first to see the increase. Brokerage firms need to be sure they protect their investment and increase investor margin requirements.

profiting with the bull

Selling naked puts allows investors to benefit in all different market conditions. The term "benefit" doesn't necessarily mean profit; it could also mean limited losses. The first and most rewarding profit is in a bullish (upward) market. The intent of selling puts is not to have the stock put to you but to allow the stock to increase in value above your selected strike price. The profits that can be made in a bullish (upward) market are huge. The first step to selling naked puts in a bullish situation is to review the chart and technical analysis of both the overall market and your selected stock to determine what news will drive the market/stock up in value and if so how far.

The most rewarding bullish naked put plays are traded on stock-split companies that have a proven record of splitting. Figure 12.1 shows great technical signs for Juniper Networks (JNPR) as the stock begins its pre–stock-split run. This is a good example of when to sell higher in the money naked puts. Figure 12.2 shows that JNPR had a big pre–stock-split rally. The stock was up 30.75 six days prior to its two-for-one stock split. Figure 12.3 shows a pre-split run by Rambus Inc. (RMBS). The stock was up 63 points eight days prior to its four-for-one stock split. Figure 12.4 shows how high RMBS's stock has climbed allowing you to buy back your in-the-money options or let them expire worthless on expiration day. I've given you a few examples as an idea of how to maximize your

figure 12.1   Juniper Networks (JNPR)

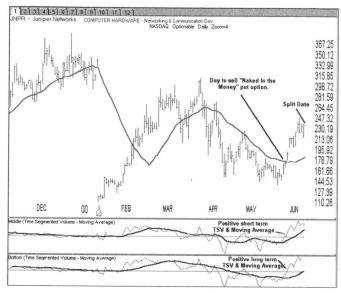

TC2000.com chart courtesy of Worden Brothers, Inc.

figure 12.2   Juniper Networks (JNPR)

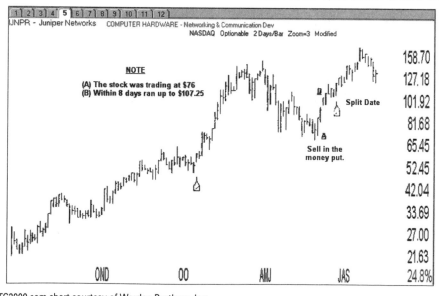

TC2000.com chart courtesy of Worden Brothers, Inc.

figure 12.3   Rambus Inc. (RMBS)

TC2000.com chart courtesy of Worden Brothers, Inc.

figure 12.4   Rambus Inc. (RMBS)

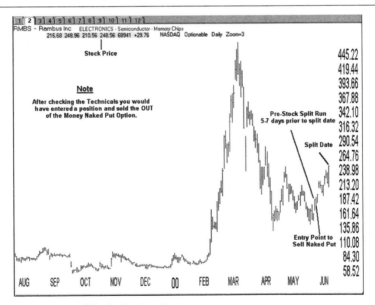

TC2000.com chart courtesy of Worden Brothers, Inc.

profits with stock-split companies. (This information is covered in detail in my book *Trade Stocks Online*.) After checking the charts and technical analysis, the next important step is selecting the right strike price to sell. Again, the chart and technical analysis for the overall market and individual stock will determine the stock's upside potential. Following is a list of five different stocks that I believe have good upside potential. As an investor, I like these stocks and would like to own them. The figures shown are from the middle of May, and the June expiration is only 14 trading days away (third Friday of the month). Let's review the option premiums and then consider which strike prices will be best based on the technical analysis and premium prices.

example 1

Company	Current Stock Price	Strike Prices	Premium
Cisco	$54.94	$50	$1.43 × $1.56
		$55	$3.12 × $3.37
		$60	$6.12 × $6.37
JDS Uniphase	$80.50	$75	$3.50 × $3.75
		$80	$5.62 × $5.87
		$85	$8.37 × $8.75
Oracle	$67	$65	$3.87 × $4.12
		$70	$6.25 × $6.62
		$75	$9.62 × $9.93
Sun Microsystems	$73.25	$70	$2.62 × $3.00
		$75	$5.00 × $5.25
		$80	$8.37 × $8.50
Nokia	$48	$45	$1.37 × $1.62
		$50	$3.50 × $3.75
		$55	$7.25 × $7.62

As you may have noticed, all five of these companies are Internet/technology stocks, which many conservative investors consider a risky investment. However, when selling naked puts, an investor must stick to the two important rules: (1) Like the stocks and be willing to own them and (2) agree to buy them at the selected strike price you chose if the stocks get put to you. I've selected these five stocks because of their technical analysis charts and the companies' past history of stock splits. All had recently split their stock. Market study shows that nine out of 10 stock-split companies return back to their previous split price within 12 to 16 months. This is a good indicator that the stocks have great upside potential.

In reviewing the three different strike prices for each stock and their offered premiums, you have to take into consideration the movement of the overall market trend. In this example, the overall market trend is bullish (upward), allowing investors to select the higher in-the-money strike prices (prices that are higher than the current stock price). With the bullish market investors are looking for stock to increase in value and be above their selected strike price on or before their selected expiration date. Figures 12.5, 12.6, 12.7, 12.8, and 12.9 show the price chart for each of the five selected stocks. By the next morning the overall direction of the stock market was bullish, as the Dow was up 127 and the Nasdaq was up 130.

figure 12.5 Cisco Systems Inc. (CSCO)

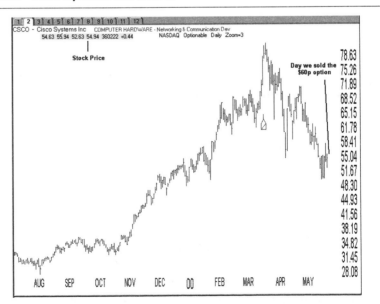

TC2000.com chart courtesy of Worden Brothers, Inc.

figure 12.6 JDS Uniphase Corp. (JDSU)

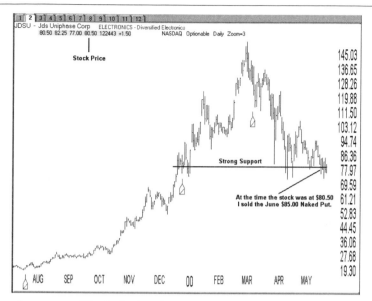

TC2000.com chart courtesy of Worden Brothers, Inc.

figure 12.7 Oracle Corporation (ORCL)

TC2000.com chart courtesy of Worden Brothers, Inc.

figure 12.8   Sun Microsystems Inc. (SUNW)

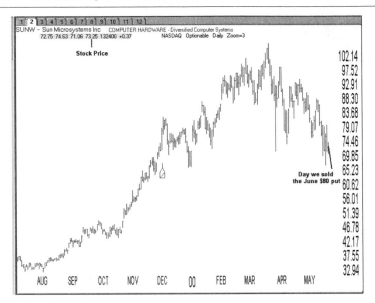

TC2000.com chart courtesy of Worden Brothers, Inc.

figure 12.9   Nokia Corp Ads (NOK)

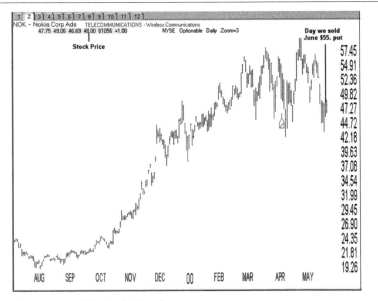

TC2000.com chart courtesy of Worden Brothers, Inc.

All five selected stocks were up in value. The out-of-the-money strike prices would have been the correct choice for a bullish market. JDSU's $85 strike price was in the money when the stock was trading at $80.50; now with the increase the stock is trading at the money. (The strike price and stock price are the same: $85.)

When selling naked put options, remember that the option premiums consist of two parts, the intrinsic value (equity) and the time value. As the stock *increases* in value, the market makers *decrease* the intrinsic value of the option, which lowers the price of the option premium. You can buy back the option (I'll explain why and how in the section "Buy Back and Roll Out") at any time as long as it is before your selected expiration date. When the stock *increases* in value, the option premium *decreases* in value, changing its original bid and ask price of $8.37 × $8.75 to $5.62 × $5.87. The difference between the original bid (selling price $8.37) and the current ask ($5.87 buying price) is $2.50. Assuming you sold 10 contracts (1,000 shares), the profit for this short-term trade would be figured by multiplying the $2.50 per share by the 1,000 shares, amounting to a profit of $2,500. Because I'm sticking to the rules of liking the stock and wanting to own it at $85 per share, I'm going to wait until the third Friday of June and then make one of three choices:

1. I will profit at expiration as option expires.
2. I will buy back put option to avoid having stock put to me.
3. Option will be exercised and stock will be put to me.

profiting at expiration

My first choice is to allow the option to expire worthless, assuming the stock is trading at $85 or higher after the market closes on the third Friday of June. When we originally sold the June $85 put option, we gave someone the right (not the obligation) to put the stock to us for $85 per share. Again, if the stock is trading at $85 or higher, then the odds are the stock will not be put to us at $85 per share. Be careful never to assume that just because the stock closed at $85 on Friday it won't get put to you. Options expire on Saturday at 12 noon following the third Friday, which still can allow time for the stock to drop in value after the close of the market on Friday. To be sure that the stock didn't get put to you, check your account on the following Monday. If the stock was not put to you, then you keep the entire premium you received when you first sold the naked put and didn't have to buy the stock. In this example, the JDSU premium received was the bid price (selling price) of $8.37. Based on 10 contracts (1,000 shares), the profit would be $8.37 × 1,000 (shares) equaling a profit of $8,370.

That's a great profit for a total of 18 days, 14 of which were trading days (days the market was open). Most investors aren't concerned with actual days (days before expiration) and trading days (days the market's open). As naked put traders we *are* concerned because as each day passes, whether weekend or trading day, the time premium of the naked put option decreases in value, allowing investors the opportunity to allow the option to expire worthless or buy back the option for less. As the stock market is closed on Saturdays and Sundays, the time premium portion of the option erodes away. Come expiration Friday, the entire time premium has eroded, leaving only the intrinsic value if the stock is trading below your selected strike price.

If that is the case, then you can consider your second of the three choices and buy back the naked put option. Come the third Friday of June (expiration), all five stocks, CSCO, JDSU, ORCL, SUNW, and NOK, were trading above the highest selected strike price of the three shown in Example 1. Go back to Figures 12.5, 12.6, 12.7, 12.8, and 12.9 and compare the charts with Figures 12.10, 12.11, 12.12, 12.13, and 12.14. You'll notice the increase of each stock upon expiration date. Because these five stocks were trading several points or more above the in-the-money strike price, the stocks did not get put to us. We also saved more money because we didn't have to pay commissions to buy the stock. There was no need to close out the option trade because the naked put option expired worthless, as no one wanted to put the stock to us at a lesser price than what the stock was trading for in the open market.

Let's review the profit for each of the five selected stocks and see what our rate of return is. First on the list we had CSCO, which was trading at $54.93 when we sold the $60 naked put option for a pre-

figure 12.10   Cisco Systems Inc. (CSCO)

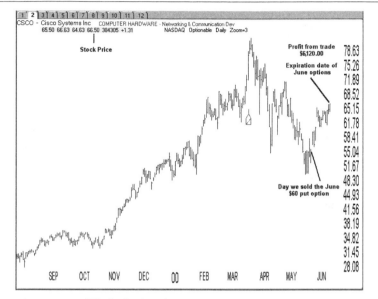

TC2000.com chart courtesy of Worden Brothers, Inc.

figure 12.11   JDS Uniphase Corp. (JDSU)

TC2000.com chart courtesy of Worden Brothers, Inc.

figure 12.12   Oracle Corporation (ORCL)

TC2000.com chart courtesy of Worden Brothers, Inc.

figure 12.13   Sun Microsystems Inc. (SUNW)

TC2000.com chart courtesy of Worden Brothers, Inc.

figure 12.14 Nokia Corp. Ads (NOK)

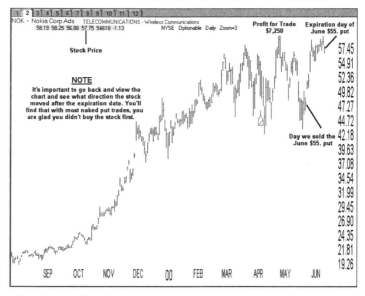

TC2000.com chart courtesy of Worden Brothers, Inc.

mium of $6.12 per share. And at the close of expiration Friday CSCO was trading at $67¹³/₁₆. Assuming in all of these examples we sold 10 contracts (1,000 shares), what was our profit and rate of return for CSCO? Because the option expired worthless as the stock was trading at $67¹³/₁₆ and we sold the $60 put option, we are entitled to keep the entire premium of $6.12 per share × 1,000 for $6,120 profit.

JDSU was trading at $120³/₁₆, and we sold the $80 naked put option when the stock was trading at $80.50. The premium received for the June $80 put option was $8.37 per share × 1,000 shares (10 contracts) for a profit of $8,370. ORCL was trading at $67 per share at the time we sold the June $75 naked put option. The premium received for that option was $9.62 per share × 1,000 shares, for $9,620 profit. Fourth on the list is SUNW, which was trading at $73.25 when we sold the June $80 naked put option. At that time we received $8.37 per share × 1,000 shares for $8,370 profit. NOK was trading at $48 per share when we sold the $55 naked put option. Again at that time we received $7.25 per share × 1,000 shares (10 contracts), for $7,250 profit. The five premium profits received equaled a grand total of $39,730. The total margin requirement is 30 percent of the actual stock price plus the total received premium of $39,730. The margin will adjust daily as the stock moves up or down.

put buy back

The second choice, come expiration or before, is to buy back the naked put option to avoid having the stock put to you. Your question at this point should be: Why? The most obvious reason is to take the profit or because the technical indicators have changed and it may not be a good time to have the stock put to you. With the change of the market volatility, a stock's future can change every day if not every minute. This is why I believe naked put options are so powerful; they allow investors several choices compared to the buying and holding of investments. When electing to buy back the put option, remember that you can do so any time after you've sold the put option, but it must be done prior to the close of the market on the third Friday of your selected month. In this example our expiration was June. As an investor I've found it more favorable to wait until the option's expiration day before buying back the naked put option.

I do this because the time premium portion of the option has eroded away, leaving just its intrinsic portion, which is the price difference between the stock's current price and the strike price of the put option you sold. Example 1 below shows the put option premium with both intrinsic and time value. Example 2 shows the put option premium after the time premium has eroded.

example 1

Stock price is trading at $83 and your option strike price is $85 with seven trading days remaining until the June expiration, and the June $85 put premium is $3^3/_4$. To determine the time premiums of the option, subtract the strike price of $85 from the current stock price of $83 equaling the intrinsic value of $2. The next step is then to subtract the current option premium of $3^3/_4$ from the intrinsic value of $2, which equals $1^3/_4$. The time premium in this example is $1^3/_4$, meaning that the option makers are allowing $1^3/_4$ of premium for the amount of time that remains between the current trading day and the expiration of the selected option on the third Friday of June.

example 2

By allowing time to erode and not buying back the put option until expiration date, the time will decay, costing you less to buy back the naked put option when closing out the position. Using the same numbers as in example 1, let's assume the stock price remained the same at $83, and it's now one hour before the expiration of the June option. Knowing that the strike price is $85 (price we agreed to have the stock put to us) and the current stock price is $83, you're left with a $2 intrinsic premium value. As for the time portion, the $1^3/_4$ premium in Example 1 was reduced as the time has eroded away, leaving about $.25 of time premium one hour before option expiration. The current option premium will now be $2.25 × 1,000 shares (10 contracts) = $2,250. Let's use the above JDSU naked put option, for which we originally received $8.37 per share × 1,000 shares (10 contracts) = $8,370. Again to determine your net profit for this trade you would subtract the premium received ($8,370) from the premium paid to buy back the put ($2,250) and you have your net profit for a short-term trade of 14 trading days: $8,370 – $2,250 = $6,120 profit.

option exercised

Reminding you of the two important rules of selling naked puts (you'd like to own the stock and at your selected strike price) brings us to the third choice of selling naked put options. It's now Monday following the third Friday of the June expiration. The stock is trading at $83 and we sold the June $85 naked put option, receiving a premium of $8,370. After checking our account on Monday following the Friday expiration, we see that the stock was put to us at the selected strike price of $85 per share. Now what does this mean? We sold someone the right to put the stock to us at $85; in doing so they paid us $8,370 to have the right to sell us 1,000 shares at the strike price ($85 per share) and it's now trading at $83. By allowing the stock to be put to us at $85 we purchased 1,000 shares of JDS Uniphase at a discounted price of $76.63 per share. Let's figure out the math and see if you agree that selling naked put options offers more opportunity than just buying the stock.

Step 1

Stock sold to us at $85 per share: $1,000 \times \$85 = \$85,000$

Current stock price $83 per share: $1,000 \times \$83 = \$83,000$

Subtract the current price: = −2,000

Step 2

Price stock was bought at: $\$85 \times 1,000 = \$85,000$

Premium received for put option: $\$8.37 \times 1,000 = \$8,370$

Stock's net price: $\$76.63 \times 1,000 = \$76,630$

When originally selling the naked put, the stock was trading at $80.50 per share, which would cost us $80,500 for 1,000 shares. Because we elected to sell the put first, allowing us the choice of having the stock put to us, we actually bought the stock at the discounted price of $76.63 per share instead of the original trading price of $80.50 per share. When we elected to have the stock put to us, we understood the risk, knowing the stock could be put to us at a lower price than our strike price. In reality, we could have bought the stock outright and it also could have dropped in value. Instead of buying the stock we elected to sell the naked put first, allowing ourselves a certain dollar amount of safety in case the stock did drop.

If, as an investor, you bought the stock at $80.50 and it dropped $5 to $75.50 you'd be unhappy and would have lost $5 per share. However, because of option investing and specialized knowledge (knowing how to sell naked puts), your cost base to own the stock is $76.63 per share, which allows the stock to drop $8.37 to $76.63 per share, losing only $1.63 per share instead of the $5 per share. The loss difference between buying the stock and first selling the naked put option saved the option investor $3.37 per share ($3.37 \times 1,000 = \$3,370$) and an opportunity to sell the stock for profit when the stock moves up above $76.63.

selling the stock

You are thankful that you sold the naked put option first and had the stock put to you at a cost of $76.63. It's now the following Monday after the June expiration and you own 1,000 shares of JDSU. What can you do now? The first question you should ask yourself is: Why did I buy the stock? And at what price would I be willing to sell the stock? As we all know, there are many different reasons why an investor invests in the stock market. If you're a long-term investor and were looking to pick up JDSU at a discounted price and did, then you may consider holding on to the 1,000 shares you bought. Or you may elect to sell a portion or all of the stock when it runs up in value.

My first choice would be to buy back the naked put option and keep the profit of the premium unless the stock/market closed with bullish signs. In that case I may consider holding the stock for a few days and then selling it to gain a larger profit. Remember, I treat the stock market as a business and take profits when I see fit. I'm not a long-term investor waiting to sell my investments when I retire or when I'm in desperate need of the money; I buy and sell naked put options to generate a monthly income. This enables me to continuously bring in a monthly income and still limit my downside, allowing me to invest each month according to market direction.

profiting with the bear

Knowing that investors with knowledge invest in a bearish market, option market makers have a tendency to inflate the put premium prices for consideration of downward market directions. As you've read earlier, investors can short a stock or in a less expensive way buy a put option that enables them to profit as the stock decreases in value.

Knowing this, option market makers always want to protect their investment when a bearish sign may be appearing so they inflate put option premiums, costing investors more money to buy a put option. For investors who rely on technical charts, these inflated options are a great opportunity to *sell* the naked put option. The first step is to research the chart and determine the stock's Support Level. This is the point at which you as the investor are confident that the stock has tested its lower price range and looks to be changing its direction from a bearish (downward) movement to a bullish (upward) movement. When looking to be conservative, investors sell naked put options by utilizing the at-the-money or out-of-the-money strike prices.

Again, don't get put and call option strike prices confused. When selling an out-of-the-money strike price for a put option, the stock price is trading higher than your selected strike price. In this example let's use the stock Nokia (NOK). Using our previous example of Nokia, the stock was trading at $48 per share and we were viewing the $45, $50, and $55 strike prices. Because the stock is trading at $48 per share, this would make the $45 strike price the out-of-the-money option. This would be the most conservative choice of the three different strike prices because it allows for the stock to *decrease* in value; with the $50 and $55 strike prices, the stock has to *increase* in value. The $45 strike price allows for a decrease of the stock's value by $3 per share; the difference of $48 (stock price) and $45 (selected strike price) equals the $3. Besides the $3 price reduction, investors also have the premium collected at the time the naked put option was sold.

Using the same price premiums as mentioned earlier, the investor received $1.37 per share for the option. This would now allow the investor a net base of $43.63 per share, meaning that the stock can drop from its current price of $48 to $43.63 per share without the investor losing any money. If the investor had bought the stock at $48 per share, he or she would have lost $4.37 per share. Multiply the $4.37 × 1,000 shares (10 contracts) for a loss of $4,370. Once again, when selling the naked put option on a stock that you'd like to own, you can control your losses by receiving the initial premium when you sell the naked put. To avoid a larger loss in examples like this one, you still can buy back the naked put option and prevent the stock from being put to you at $45. Doing this allows for some degree of loss in case the market or individual stock changes directions from bullish to bearish.

buy back and roll out

The phrase "buy back and roll out" is exactly what occurs when a naked put trade has gone against you. To help you fully understand this concept, I'll need to start at the beginning of the trade and follow through step by step. For this example I'm going to use an actual trade that was placed on a company known as Power Integrations, Inc. (POWI). At the time I elected to sell the naked put on the stock the stock was trading at about $25 per share. Now remember the two rules of selling naked put options: (1) You must like the stock (meaning you're willing to buy it) and (2) you're willing to buy the stock at the strike price you sold the naked put for. With this thought in mind, I decided to sell 10 contracts (1,000 shares) of the March 25p (put) at a price of $2.25 per share. The total premium I took in was $2,250 ($2.25 × 1,000 shares). Now all I was looking for was the stock to remain above the selected strike price ($25) come the third Friday of March. If so I make $2,250 and didn't have to buy the stock.

Keep in mind that the stock was trading at $25. If I were to buy the stock, 1,000 shares would have cost me $25,000 ($25 × 1,000). But because I sold the naked put first I was spending only $9,750 (30 percent of the stock price [$7,500] plus the received premium of $2,250 instead of $25,000). I'm explaining "buy back with a rollout" in detail so that you can see how I survived a market that went from bullish to bearish and took out over one-third of the investors. Because I entered a trade allowing some room for a correction (premium I received by selling the naked put first), I was able to react to the market change and turn a losing position into a profit. Here's how. I was anticipating that the stock would not only stay above $25 but go even higher, as the technical indicators showed a strong Balance of Power, TSV, and Stochastics that were crossing over to the upside on increased volume. Of the many technical indicators, these three showed a strong bullish signal, giving me high anticipation of the stock's upward movement. But then came our stock market friend, the "trend."

Remember the saying "Make the market trend your friend"? I was in a bullish trade and then came April and the Dow Jones dropped 374 points and the next day the Nasdaq dropped 200 points. The bullish trend had now become a bearish trap, as investors were selling stock fast. The change from buying to selling is known as a trend reversal, which alerted me to take action. As the market was selling off, the $25 stock had dropped to about $21. I reacted by buying back the April $25 naked put option for a price of $5 per share and then rolling out to the next month of May and then selling the $25 naked put again, now receiving $6 per share. Now that I have you confused, let's do the math. Originally when I sold the April 25p (put) I received $2.25 per share multiplied by 1,000 shares (10 contracts) for $2,250. The next step was to buy back *exactly* what I sold, the April 25p (put) for the current ask price of $5 per share × 1,000 shares (10 contracts) = $5,000.

Because I had to spend $5,000 and received only $2,250 I was negative $2,750. I have just covered the buy-back portion of a rollout, which stops anyone from putting the stock to me at $25 per share. When buying back a naked put option, be sure you always buy back the *exact* strike price and month of the option you sold. If you don't you will have created a worse situation and will be holding on to two different naked put trades. Don't laugh. I've seen people make this mistake. Instead of closing out a trade they accidentally opened a second trade. It must be the *exact month* and *strike price*.

roll out

Now that you've closed out the naked put by buying back the exact month and strike price, you can reenter the trade by selling the next month out. In this example we're going to sell the May put option. But at what strike price? Originally you sold the $25 strike price. Now that the stock has dropped, you may consider dropping down to the next lower strike price. In this example I resold the same $25 strike price again. Why would someone sell a naked put on a stock that went against him or her? I did so because I like the stock and I wouldn't mind owning it at a price of $25 per share. There's your answer, again the rules to selling naked put options. Also remember the technical analyses were good and the stock has great upside potential. It was just a hostage of the selloff of the Dow Jones and Nasdaq indexes.

Just minutes after I bought back my original April $25p (put) I was free of the obligation for April so I decided to take advantage of the downsided market. I decided to allow time to work for me instead of against me, which is why I sold the May $25p (put). By closing out the April $25 put and reselling the May $25, I give the stock more time to go from the bearish price of $21 back above my elected strike price of $25. I allowed time to work for me, not against me when I rolled out of the April $25 put and resold the May $25 put. Now that you have a basic understanding of buy back and roll out, let's complete the math and show you the profit.

Originally
Sold the April $25 put for $2.25 per share × 1,000 shares = $2,250 into my account.

Buy Back
Bought back the April $25 put for $5 per share × 1,000 shares = $5,000 out of my account. Now negative $2,750 on this trade.

Roll Back In
Sell the May $25 put for $6 per share × 1,000 shares = $6,000 into my account.

Close Out Trade
Stock closes at $25.50 and doesn't get put to me so my naked put option expires worthless and I keep the entire $6,000.

Trading Profit
Profit is figured by adding the two received put premiums together and then subtracting the put premium paid to buy back the April put.

1. Received $2,250 when selling the April put.
2. Received $6,000 when selling the May put.
3. Paid $5,000 when buying back the April put (roll out).
4. Total received was $8,250 – $5,000 = $3,250 profit.

How does selling naked puts benefit an option investor compared to just an investor who buys the stock outright? Because option investors sell naked puts first, they are given several advantages compared to an investor who bought the stock. I've explained these advantages throughout this chapter, so be sure you understand not only the advantages but the disadvantages also. With the example of Power Integrations, Inc. (POWI), the stock could have been purchased in the beginning of April for $25 per share ($25,000) and was only trading at $25.50 ($25,500) three weeks into May. Investors who had bought the stock would have realized a gain of only $500. The option investor was the true winner as he realized a gain of $3,250, which is a net difference of $2,750 between the two different investment opportunities.

At times of uncertainty or in changing market conditions, review all your choices as an investor to select the strategy that will meet both your needs and the condition of the market. Naked put options have become extremely popular over the last several years. As the market experiences higher highs and lower lows along with an extreme amount of volatility, investors are taking more conservative positions first. Consider naked put options as a way of insuring your investments as you would your home or car. For more information and education tools about writing put options, visit www.writingputs.com.

Chapter 12 Quiz

1. In the phrase "writing naked put options," the term "writing" means:

   a. buying   b. shorting   c. selling

2. What are the two rules you must never break when writing naked put options?

   a. You must like the stock.

   b. You must be willing to buy it at the selected strike price.

   c. You must have at least 50 percent of the strike price in your account.

3. The term "naked" means you don't own the underlying stock yet you have the ability to sell it.

   a. true   b. false

4. If a stock is trading at $60 and you elected to sell an in-the-money naked put option, which one of the three prices would be considered the in-the-money option?

   a. $55   b. $60   c. $65

5. When selling naked put options, the largest profit gained is when the stock price is trading _____ your selected strike price upon expiration.

   a. below   b. at   c. above

6. You've sold a June $65 naked put option and come the day of the expiration, the stock is trading at $63. You have three choices by the close of the market: You can buy back the naked option you sold, you can allow the stock to be put to you at the price of $65 per share, or you can implement a buy back with a roll-out strategy.

   a. true   b. false

7. Writing naked put options is very risky, and investors would be much better off if they were to buy and hold stocks long term.

   a. true   b. false   c. sometimes

8. If you choose to sell a naked put option, can you close out your position win or lose prior to its expiration date?

   a. yes   b. sometimes   c. no

9. The ideal time frame when selling naked put options is _____ days prior to the next expiration of options.

   a. 30   b. 60   c. 90

10. Selling naked put options gives an investor the ability to make money when the stock price goes up in value, stays the same in value, or drops in value.

    a. true   b. false

Chapter 12 Quiz Answers

1. The term "writing" means *selling*. The term is commonly used with selling naked puts and covered calls. Both of these "writing" strategies are option investments.

2. The two rules you must never break when writing naked puts options are: *you must like the stock* and be willing to own it, and *you must be willing to buy it at the selected strike price* of the option you sold. Selling naked put options gives someone the right to put the stock to you on or before the expiration date at the selected strike price you chose.

3. *True.* The stock market term "naked" simply means that you have sold someone the right to put the stock to you at the selected strike price you've chosen. For this right the person must pay you a fee. I refer to the fee as an insurance premium the owner of the stock must pay for the right to force the stock to you.

4. The correct answer is the *$65* strike price. Remember that the put option terms in, at, and out of the money are the opposite of when trading call options. If the stock was trading at $60, then the $60 strike price is known as at the money; the $55 is out of the money; and it's the $65 strike price that is in the money by $5 (the difference between the strike price and the current stock price).

5. Ideally when selling naked put options, investors' largest profit is when the stock price is trading *above* their selected strike price upon the expiration of the option. Because the stock is trading above the selected strike price, the option will expire worthless as the seller of the stock doesn't have the right to put the stock to you. Only when the stock is trading below your strike price does the stock owner have the right to force the sale of the stock to you.

6. *True.* You have several choices. The ideal choice would be to buy back the exact option strike price and month you sold and keep the difference between what the buyback cost is

and the premium you received when you first sold the naked put option. By doing so you've closed out the position and received a short-term profit. The other two choices are considered *only* if the stock has dropped much lower than your selected strike price.

7. *False*. However, because of the lack of understanding of naked put options, most people still relate the term "risk" with any option strategy. Selling the naked put first allows you the opportunity to buy the stock at a discounted price or limit your losses if the stock was to drop in value. This is a wiser choice than buying the stock outright and then losing money as it drops.

8. *Yes*. When selling a naked put option or trading any option, remember the definition of an option. You have the "right" on or "before" expiration to buy or sell stocks for a "certain" price. It's wise to close out your option position if one of two things occur during your option time frame. First, the stock runs up above your selected strike and the premium has dropped. If this happens, buy back the option and keep your profit. Second, the technical chart shows good indications that the stock may complete a reversal pattern and have a large drop in price. By buying back the option, you close out the position and stop anyone from selling the stock to you at a much higher price than what it may be worth.

9. When selling naked put options, it's always been my experience to go out only *30* days to the next option expiration date. By trying to sell options farther out than 30 days, you're increasing your odds and allowing for more to occur. With today's market volatility, it's much riskier to allow more time to work against you and not for you. This investment strategy is designed to generate a *monthly* income, giving you the choice to roll out to the next month if the investment didn't perform as planned.

10. *True*. You can make money when the stock goes up, stays the same, or drops in value. This is the largest misunderstanding about writing puts. You benefit in all three situations:

A. If the stock is above your selected strike price upon expiration, you keep the entire premium you received when you first sold the put option.

B. If the stock is trading at the same price as when you sold the naked put option, you close out the position and buy back the same option, which allows you to keep the remaining premium. There will always be a profit because options consist of two parts: equity (there is none if the stock and strike price are the same) and premium (which erodes away as the option gets closer to expiration).

C. If the stock has dropped within the amount of the premium you received, you can do one of three things:

(1) Buy back the option, which costs you the premium you received. Yet you didn't lose any money.

(2) Buy back the option and roll out to the next month and receive the premium again.

(3) Allow the stock to be put to you at a discounted price. Because you sold the put option first, you received a premium limiting your losses.

chapter 13

investment structuring

The first and most important step to investing properly begins when an investor opens the proper investment account. Many investors have found corporate investment accounts to offer more advantages over the standard sole proprietorship account. The largest overlooked question for investors is how to structure the stock (investment) trading account. Should investments be traded in a personal account, a family limited partnership, an inter vivos trust, a partnership, a limited liability company (LLC), or a corporation?

Of all these types of business entities, a corporation will give you the greatest benefits. A *properly structured* corporation will protect assets, provide nontaxable perks, permit tax savings, and provide you with liability protection.

Federal tax laws apply equally to all privately held corporations, regardless of their state of domicile. Retirement benefits, business deductions, federal tax rates, and other permissible corporate benefits are available to all corporations. However, not all states provide the same corporate protections and benefits. For instance, most states have a corporate income tax. Some states (e.g., California and New York) are voracious in their tax collection efforts. Only a handful of states, such as Nevada, have no corporate state income taxes. Different states provide different levels of protection for the stockholders of a corporation. Stockholders, as a general rule, are not responsible for the debts of the corporation beyond their investment in the corporation. However, all states permit creditors to attempt to "pierce the corporate veil" and hold stockholders liable for the debts of the corporation. Nevada is one of the toughest states in which to attempt to pierce the corporate veil. States provide different levels of corporate confidentiality. Some states require full disclosure of all officers, directors, and stockholders of privately held corporations. Other states, such as Nevada, do not require public disclosure of the stockholders.

Carefully determine which corporate structure and domicile is best for your situation. Here are some questions to ask yourself:

- Are you trying to protect your assets?
- Are you using your corporation to operate a business in your home state?
- Are you using your corporation to operate a business nationally or internationally?
- Are you using your corporation to develop a viable retirement program?
- Are you using your corporation to develop an estate plan thereby reducing your potential estate taxes? (Estate taxes begin at 37 percent and increase to 55 percent, with a surcharge on top of that.)
- Are you using your corporation to trade in the stock market?

All of these questions must be answered before the corporation is formed. But, make no mistake about it, by properly forming and operating a corporation, you can protect your assets and, in most cases, substantially reduce your tax burden.

why a Nevada corporation?

Where should you incorporate? In 1987 Nevada revised its corporate statutes, making it the most favorable state in the nation. It is now Nevada, not Delaware, that is the more desirable state in which to incorporate a privately held corporation. (Delaware is still the better state for a publicly held corporation, for Delaware law permits corporations to utilize strong anti-takeover provisions, some of which are prohibited in Nevada.)

The following are some reasons to form a privately held corporation in Nevada. (Remember, some of these benefits are available to all corporations, not just those domiciled in Nevada.)

- Nevada is extremely "pro-corporation." It enacted new corporate statutes in 1987, strongly favoring the establishment of privately held corporations in Nevada. In 1998 Nevada ranked among the top 10 states in the country in new corporate filings. This puts it right up there with such states as New York, California, and Delaware.

- It is almost impossible to "pierce the corporate veil" in Nevada. Piercing the corporate veil is a legal strategy whereby a creditor can penetrate the corporate entity and obtain satisfaction of a judgment directly from the corporate stockholders. The Nevada courts have consistently denied plaintiffs the right to pierce the corporate veil, even when other states would have granted the request.

- A corporation has a much lower tax rate than individuals. A corporation pays U.S. federal income tax of only 15 percent on the first $50,000 ($7,500), and only 22.25 percent on the first $100,000 ($22,250) of taxable income.

- According to the *Wall Street Journal*, in 1992 the Internal Revenue Service estimated that 56.8 percent of the "underreported" taxes came from small businesses, *which do not include corporations*. "C" corporations are less likely to be audited by the IRS than sole proprietorships, Subchapter S corporations, or independent contractors.

- Nevada has no state personal income taxes, no state corporate income taxes, no franchise taxes, no taxes on corporate shares, no transfer taxes, and no succession taxes, and its corporate filing fees are among the lowest in the United States. Even Delaware now imposes a franchise tax on corporations domiciled in that state.

- The transactions and meetings of a privately held Nevada corporation are truly "private." There is no requirement to publicly report any such meetings. Delaware corporations, for example, are required to publish the date, time, and place of the annual stockholders' meeting.

- Corporations can deduct 100 percent of their employees' medical benefits, including medical insurance premiums, from their pretax profits. (Currently, self-employed people can deduct only 30 percent of their health insurance premiums as a business expense. All other deductions must be taken on Schedule A of their 1040 forms.) A corporate medical benefits plan must be available to all employees of the corporation. Thus, a properly structured Nevada corporation will have only you and your family under the plan and can provide you with a much more comprehensive plan, all of which is tax deductible.

- A corporation can provide a "defined benefits" retirement package for its employees. A self-employed individual is limited to a "defined payments" retirement package, such as an IRA or a 401(k) plan, which limit the amount that can be contributed annually. (Note: Retirement plans normally result in tax-deferred income to the recipient, but neither the corporation nor the recipient pays taxes on contributions to the plan.) As with the medical plan, the retirement plan must be available to all employees (although a two-tier plan is available for the officers of the corporation). Again, the benefits of a Nevada corporation are obvious, for a properly structured Nevada corporation will have only you and/or your spouse as the sole beneficiaries of this retirement plan, permitting a more flexible plan to be put into operation.

- There are minimal reporting requirements in Nevada. Only the names and business addresses of the officers and directors need be disclosed to the state. Stockholders of a Nevada corporation are not a matter of public record.

- Nevada truly permits a "one-person" corporation. One person can hold the required offices of president, secretary, and treasurer of the corporation, and also be its sole director, thereby satisfying all the disclosure laws of Nevada. Vice president of the corporation does not have to be named or identified at any time.

- Nevada permits the board of directors meetings to be held anywhere in the world. Travel and expenses for the meetings are tax deductible by the corporation and are not income for the board member.

- Stockholders, officers, and directors of a Nevada corporation are not required to live in Nevada, nor are they required to be U.S. citizens.

- Nevada has stronger laws protecting officers and directors from liability for acts done either by the corporation or on behalf of the corporation than any other state. Nevada is the only state that requires a showing of "gross negligence," a legal burden extremely hard to meet.

- A properly formed Nevada corporation will permit stock trading without the IRS holding it to be a "personal holding corporation" with its correspondingly high taxes.

- Nevada is the only state in the United States that does not have a reciprocal information sharing agreement with the IRS.

- A Nevada corporation can provide asset protection and be utilized for personal estate preservation.

would *your* situation benefit from a Nevada corporation?

Clearly, Nevada offers a host of benefits over every other state. The main question to ask yourself is: How does it apply to my situation? Let's cover some common reasons why people incorporate in the state of Nevada.

situation 1: a new business with a presence in your home state

You are starting a new business. You have decided that it makes more sense to incorporate as opposed to acting as a sole proprietorship or a general partnership. You incorporate in Nevada and now have the limited liability protection and tax advantages of a Nevada corporation. For purposes of discussion, let's assume you reside in California and want to open a restaurant in Malibu. Can your Nevada corporation own and operate that business? Yes, it can, although that may not be the best way to go.

general rule 1: it makes no difference where you live

Your state of residence has no effect on whether you incorporate in Nevada or any other state. However, if you take a salary from the corporation, you will have to pay required personal taxes on that income in *your state of residence.*

Ask yourself the following questions:

- Does your business have a physical presence in your home state?
- Does your business have an office in your home state?
- Does it have a local phone number?
- Does it have a mailing address?
- Has it been issued a business license in your home state?
- Do customers come to your business location?
- Does your business advertise locally?
- Does it pay local property taxes, sales taxes, and employment taxes?

If the answer is *yes* to one or more of these questions, then your business may have a physical presence in that state, such as your restaurant in Malibu.

If the answers are *no*, then you have two choices:

1. Form a Nevada corporation first and then register it as a foreign corporation in your home state. If you choose to go this route, you will lose some of the benefits a Nevada corporation has to offer. A Nevada corporation will be subject to the laws of the state in which it is doing business. Thus, even though Nevada is the most difficult state in the country to pierce the corporate veil and go after the stockholders personally, the laws of the local jurisdiction may well be applied and this protection may be substantially reduced. However, Nevada does provide greater privacy and confidentiality in the structuring

of its domestic corporations. These benefits will carry over to the other states and will be respected by the courts.

2. Incorporate in the home state and save the additional paper-work and filing fees.

Recommendation: If you are doing business in the local markets only, then incorporate in your home state. If you are doing business around the country, incorporate in Nevada. Even if you choose to incorporate in your home state (as would be the case in the restaurant example), there are still powerful reasons to add a Nevada corporation to the strategy. We will look at these later.

situation 2: a new business that could be based anywhere

You are opening up a new company that sells products for a direct sales company. You are either conducting sales over the Internet or traveling around the country selling the products and building a team to do the same. You work out of your home and do not have an office.

general rule 1

If your business can be based anywhere and you form a Nevada cor-poration *properly*, you will be able to take advantage of *everything* a Nevada corporation has to offer!

general rule 2

In order to *properly* form a corporation in Nevada to serve your cus-tomers, the corporation should have, at a minimum, the following:

- A corporation formed in Nevada and current with the secretary of state
- A Nevada bank account
- A Nevada physical and mailing address
- A Nevada telephone number
- A Nevada business license (if required)
- A Nevada office
- Payment of all federal income taxes and all federal, state, and local payroll and business taxes and license fees

Now you have a presence in Nevada for your new direct sales company. It is important to note that *all* of these items are essential to establish a properly structured Nevada corporation doing business within the state of Nevada.

situation 3: incorporated in your home state but seeking lower state taxes

Let us assume that your California restaurant earns $100,000 in annual net profits as a California corporation. The corporation will have to pay 9.7 percent in California state tax for a total of $9,700. Assume you formed a separate Nevada corporation and the California corporation hired it (the Nevada corporation) to take over its marketing at $5,000 per month. Now, $60,000 of the $100,000 net profit would be transferred over to the Nevada corporation where there is no state corporate tax. In this example, you will *save over $5,820* in state taxes alone!

general rule 1

You must form a Nevada corporation properly (as in Situation 2) allowing you to have a viable corporation that can transact business with your home state corporation/business.

general rule 2

The marketing company (Nevada corporation) must have a contract with the California company. Invoices *must* be sent each month to validate these transactions. There should also be appropriate corporate resolutions granting this action by the corporation.

general rule 3

"Form over substance." The first part of this equation is met when you properly form the Nevada corporation. The Nevada corporation should also have the proper substance so it can stand up to any legal questioning of its existence. Forming the corporation alone would not stand up against legal scrutiny by a judge or an IRS examiner. Substance must be added to the equation. Substance is everything that is put in place to establish the corporate presence in Nevada as described in Situation 2. By having the proper resolutions in place, you are providing substance to your properly structured corporation. In other words, if you are considering using a Nevada corporation and do not operate it with proper substance, problems are sure to follow!

situation 4: you want to protect your assets

A Nevada corporation, properly structured, can own all of your assets. Remember, it is not necessary to own anything, as long as you have the exclusive enjoyment of it. In this scenario, you will not have anything in your name. And if you do retain assets in your name, such as your residence, the corporation can encumber them through the use of a subordinate lien (deed of trust or mortgage), thereby reducing the available equity in the asset to zero. Thus, your principal residence, for example, will no longer have anything available for a judgment creditor to seize. The same strategy can be used to encumber personal property through the use of a personal property lien (commonly called a UCC-1 form).

When a Nevada corporation is properly structured, creditors looking to seize any of your personal assets won't find much in your name and what they do find will be encumbered. Creditors may find that you hold some stock in a Nevada corporation. (That's where the assets will be placed or protected.) In a properly structured Nevada corporation, you will be a minority stockholder but will have total control of the corporation. At the judgment debtor hearing, you can truthfully reveal that you own a small amount of stock in the corporation. Because it is a minority interest, it has no value. As such, your creditors probably will not be interested in the stock. But even if they are, you still control the corporation and can move the assets, if necessary. Most likely, however, the creditors would move on to other assets they can seize with greater ease, and the bulk of your assets will remain protected in the Nevada corporation.

situation 5: trading stocks through your corporation

A corporation can do almost anything an individual can. For example, it can:

- Own assets
- Buy and sell assets
- Maintain a stock trading account in its own name

If you want to actively participate in the investment markets, it makes sense to do so through a corporation. The account is in the corporation's name, and you will act only as the designated trader of the corporation. When acting as the designated trader on behalf of the corporation, you may be entitled as an employee to receive benefits such as:

- Travel expenses
- Car allowance
- Medical coverage
- Salary
- Employee bonus

All brokerage firms vary in their requirements. Some brokerage firms may require you (the designated trader) to be an officer of the corporation. A properly maintained Nevada corporation will permit this and still maintain the confidential identity of the elected trader. This properly formed corporation can trade investments and not be considered a personal holding corporation by the IRS.

general rule 1
If the IRS found an improperly structured corporation to be a personal holding corporation, the corporation would be assessed a flat tax of 39 percent on its income. A personal holding corporation is one that has five or fewer stockholders owning 50 percent or more of the voting stock *and* 60 percent or more of its income is "personal holding company" income. If the corporation fails to meet either prong of this test, it is not a personal holding corporation.

situation 6: you want privacy
You either want to set up your new business discreetly or want to get your assets out of your name. Keep in mind if you are currently involved in legal battles, transferring or selling any of your assets may be viewed as fraudulent conveyance. Be careful and please consult a legal expert regarding this possibility. Asset protection planning works best if it is done before problems arise. Would you look to buy life insurance after your spouse dies? Of course not! When filing for

bankruptcy, debtors must state if they have transferred or sold any assets within the last year. In other words, if you are planning to transfer assets out of your own name and then declare personal bankruptcy a week later, this will cause problems. Consult with a bankruptcy attorney in this case.

general rule 1

When we speak of privacy, the goal is to help lower your profile. It's not having something to hide, but rather making it more difficult for others to sue and claim what you worked to attain. Could you locate all of Rockefeller's assets? No way! His attorneys probably have a hard time locating everything.

general rule 2

If you are interested in privacy, then use one or more privately held Nevada corporations. Situations 1 to 6 are the most common situations people must face when deciding to incorporate. Your situation may be a slight variation of one of the preceding versions. Other entities may be used to further protect your assets, such as a limited partnership, an inter vivos revocable trust (commonly called a Family Living Trust), or a limited liability company (LLC). All of these other entities have some flaws but can be used very effectively with one or more Nevada corporations to protect your assets.

The information in this chapter is provided to help investors understand the difference between investing as a sole proprietor and treating your investments like a business. There is no reason why we as individual investors should not take advantage of the wonderful benefits that are offered to those who incorporate. Our government has allowed such tax advantages to corporations, yet they have failed to communicate these advantages to the individual investor. As individual investors we have been taught that buying and holding our investments long term offers greater rewards. While this statement may be true, investors don't consider that our economy will continue to change, as will the inflation rates, creating higher tax brackets in the future. An example of a government investment program is a 401(k) plan, which allows you to defer your tax dollars until the investment is withdrawn. However, you are left with the uncertainty of two important key factors:

1. Penalty for early withdrawal of funds
2. Deferred taxes to a later time with an unknown tax rate

The government created 401(k) investment plans because the current Social Security system does not look promising for the future. I'm in favor of 401(k) plans when employers offer assistance ("match" percentage given by employer when employee invests) to the plan. But still, investors have to be concerned with how much control they have over the investments.

A properly structured 401(k) investment plan within your corporation provides better tax advantages and personal control of your investments, allowing for controlled tax obligations without early withdrawal penalties. Most 401(k) plans that are set up today are not self-directed, which limits ability to implement different investment opportunities. Investors need to understand that what they do now will determine what they can do when they retire. Properly planning for the future of your family begins with the proper knowledge. Don't let time pass you by and wait until it's too late. Plan your retirement today and reap the rewards later.

As the Social Security fund stands now, the average retired person will receive about $1,250 per month, not tax-free. Now I'm sure that will change as we approach the retirement era, as the baby boomers will be the largest group to ever qualify for Social Security. There will be less money going in to the program than money going out.

The biggest problem with our government program is that congressional officials don't pay into Social Security. They don't invest into the program and they don't collect from the program. Well, how do they survive after leaving office? Let's just use the term "well off."

Social Security wasn't good enough for congressional officials, so they created and passed their own retirement plan many years ago. For all practical purposes it works like this: When they retire or leave office, they continue to draw the same pay until they die. (They occasionally receive increases as the cost of living increases.) Where does their retirement (free money) come from? From the government's general fund, the same tax account we all pay our taxes into. That's right, it's our *tax* money that allows congressional officials to carry on the same lifestyle until death. *Now* it is clearer why someone would want to be in politics! It may not be the greatest job, but it offers a great retirement plan.

We the people of this country can't vote on our own government retirement plan, but we can treat our investments as a business and limit our taxes and liability. As a resident of California I was excited to learn that as of January 2000, the estate tax level was raised from $600,000 to $625,000. The part I didn't like was the tax rate, which also rose, from 50 percent to 55 percent. What this simply means is that if I elect to live and die in the state of California and my entire assets exceed $625,000, I have to pay Uncle Sam 55 percent for every penny above the $625,000. I bring this to your attention to make you think about planning for your future and the future of your assets.

If you are interested in taking advantage of the tremendous benefits that Nevada corporations offer, call Corporate Support Services of Nevada (CSS Nevada) and they will be able to guide you in the right direction to planning for a better retirement: 1-877-5NV-CORP (1-877-568-2677).

Chapter 13 Quiz

1. Of the three choices, which *one* choice offers an investor more benefits when utilizing an investment account?

   a. individual account   b. corporation   c. family trust

2. A Nevada corporation can maintain an investment account for both the corporate officers and company employees.

   a. true   b. false

3. With a Nevada corporation, it is almost impossible for anyone to pierce the corporate veil and receive a satisfactory judgment against the shareholders.

   a. true   b. false

4. A Nevada corporation cannot be used as a form of asset protection or personal preservation.

   a. true   b. false

5. What percentage of medical insurance and premiums can be deducted as a Nevada corporation?

   a. 30 percent   b. 55 percent   c. 100 percent

6. Of the three different types of corporate officers found in most corporations, which *one* is *not* required or disclosed by the state of Nevada?

   a. president   b. vice president   c. secretary

7. A Nevada corporation can pay the investment manager (you) as well as such expenses as: newspapers, fax machine, phone lines, traveling expenses, automobile-related costs, cellular phone, and a salary and/or bonuses.

   a. true   b. false

8. A Nevada corporation must have a business located in the state of Nevada in order to utilize the advantages offered.

   a. true   b. false

9. A Nevada corporation that manages a retirement plan for its corporate officers and/or employees must utilize the services of *only* a Nevada-based investment firm.

   a. true   b. false

10. A profitable difference between a personal retirement plan and a corporate retirement plan is the tax rate. As a Nevada corporation, there are no state taxes, and the federal tax bracket is different for a corporation than it is for an individual. As an individual an investment account is taxed as personal income or long-term gains, while a corporation is taxed at a lower fixed rate. The fixed rate is 15 percent on the first $50,000. Between $50,000 and $100,000 the tax rate is _____. Above $100,000 there are other increases in the tax rate.

    a. 20 percent   b. 22$\frac{1}{4}$ percent   c. 28 percent

Chapter 13 Quiz Answers

1. Of the three choices, it's the properly structured *corporation* investment account that offers an investor different advantages. Here are a few:

   a. No state tax (Nevada)

   b. Reduced personal privacy

   c. Flexible investment opportunities (i.e., sell naked options)

   d. Lower federal tax rates

2. *True*. A corporate investment account can maintain accounts for both corporate officers and employees. This can be done with a self-directed 401(k) plan.

3. *True*. Because the corporate officers are responsible only for their share of the investment to the corporation, the liability is limited. Also, because Nevada doesn't provide the list of corporate officers to the IRS or public, piercing the corporate veil is much more difficult.

4. *False*. Some of the advantages of a Nevada corporation allow shareholders the ability to protect and preserve assets.

5. The correct answer is *100 percent*. The corporation is able to pay for all medical policies and expenses.

6. Most states require that the four corporate officers—president, vice president, secretary, and treasurer—be listed. The state of Nevada doesn't require the *vice president* to be listed on the annual statement of officers. This is another way for individuals to utilize their personal involvement with the corporation yet still remain private.

7. *True*. By treating your investments as a business and setting up the proper corporation, these costs are required business expenses related to properly managing an investment portfolio. As an individual investor these costs cannot be deducted from your investment proceeds. The largest mistake investors make is not treating their investments as a business and taking advantage of corporate benefits.

8. *False*. It is likely for a Nevada corporation to have a business located in a different state, not in Nevada. Again, the most important aspect of the corporation is properly structuring it to meet your business needs. Refer to the California restaurant example in this chapter.

9. *False*. The investment account for the corporation doesn't have to be located in the state of Nevada. The corporation may elect to have an investment account in any state.

10. The major advantage of having a corporate investment account is paying lower taxes. Individual investors pay 28 percent to 32 percent for federal taxes and then the required state taxes (average 8 percent) in which they reside. A Nevada corporation pays only 15 percent on the first $50,000 and only $22\frac{1}{4}$ percent up to $100,000, and *no* state tax. Also remember that the corporation can deduct all the associated expenses and individual investors can't deduct any associated expenses or losses.

glossary

ask price the current price for which a security may be bought (purchased).

asset allocation how assets are diversified between various investments: stocks, bonds, real estate, etc.

at the close the last price a security trades for, when the market stops trading for the day.

at the money an option whose strike price is the same as the stock price.

at the open the price a stock security trades for, when the market begins trading for the day.

Balance of Power (BOP) a technical indicator developed by Worden Brothers designed to show patterns of systematic buying and selling by informed buyer.

bearish a trading environment when the market is declining.

bear spread in futures and options trading, a strategy in which one contract is bought and a different contract is sold in such a manner that the person undertaking the spread makes a profit if the price of the underlying asset declines.

bell the device that sounds to mark the open and close of each trading day on an organized securities exchange.

best ask the price at which market makers who own a security offer to sell it; also known as the ask price. The lowest quoted offer price of all competing market makers to sell a particular stock at any given time.

bid price the current price at which you could sell your security. The bid is the side where market makers are willing to buy a security. Commonly it's always lower then the asking price.

bid/ask spread the difference between the price at which a market maker is willing to buy a security (bid) and the price at which the firm is willing to sell it (ask). The spread narrows or widens according to the supply and demand for the security being traded.

Black Monday a widely used reference to October 19, 1987, the day the Dow Jones Industrial Average dropped a record 508 points, nearly 23 percent.

Black Thursday a widely used reference to October 24, 1929, the date on which security prices plunged, producing one of the most memorable days in the history of the New York Stock Exchange.

block trade usually, a trade of 10,000 shares or more. For bonds a $200,000 face amount or more. Block trades are often executed through a special section of a brokerage firm called the block desk. Using the block desk may result in a better price.

board of directors the group of people responsible for supervising the affairs of a corporation. This group is also responsible for the decision of splitting the company stock.

bottom fishing used to refer to the activity of investing in securities when it is believed the market has reached bottom following a major decline.

breakaway gap in technical terms, a gap in a chart pattern of price movement indicating a stock price has broken out of a trend on high volume.

break-out the advance of a stock price above a Resistance Level, or the fall of a stock price below a Support Level.

broker an individual or firm that brings together buyers and sellers but does not take a position in the asset to be exchanged. In the broadest sense, an agent who facilitates trades between a buyer and a seller and receives a commission for those services.

bullish relating to the belief that a particular stock or the overall market as a whole is headed for a period of generally rising prices.

bull spread in futures and options trading, a strategy in which one contract is bought and a different contract is sold in such a manner that the person undertaking the spread makes a profit if the price of the underlying asset rises. Two contracts are used in order to limit the size of the potential loss. Bull spreads are used for both call and put options.

buying power the funds in an investor's brokerage account that may be used for purchasing securities. An investor's buying power includes cash balances plus the loan value on securities held in the account

buy signal an indication provided by a technical tool, such as a bar chart or trading volume, that a particular security or securities in general should be purchased.

buy stop order a customer's order to a broker to buy a security if it sells at or above a stipulated stop price. This type of stop order can be used to protect an existing profit or to limit the potential loss on a security that has been sold short.

call option an option contract, giving the owner the right (not the obligation) to buy shares of stock at a certain strike price on or before the expiration date. The investor has the right to also sell the option for a profit before the expiration of the option. The buyer of the underlying stock is speculating that the stock will go up in value, hence increasing the value of the option.

called away stock taken (sold) away from option seller because stock was at or above the strike price on the third Friday of the expiration month.

call price the price investors pay when purchasing the call option giving them the right to buy stock for a certain price (alsŏ known as the premium) on or before the expiration date of the chosen option.

call spread the result of an investor buying a call on a particular security and writing a call with a different expiration date, different exercise price, or both on the same security.

canceled order a customer order to a broker that cancels an earlier, unfilled order given by the customer. A canceled order can be used when buying or selling.

cash account an account in which a client is required to pay in full for securities purchased by a specific date from the trade date. Cleared funds must be in the account within three business days to cover any purchases.

channeling stock stock/index that trades up and down in a pattern between its support and Resistance Level.

chasing a stock buying or shorting a stock after it has already made a large move. Chasing a stock is considered very dangerous, because one may buy at the top or short the stock at the bottom.

Chicago Board Options Exchange (CBOE) a securities exchange established in 1973 as the nation's first organized floor for trading standardized options. Although its success spawned option trading on a number of other exchanges, the CBOE remains the most active options exchange in the country.

circuit breaker a procedure that temporarily halts trading on all U.S. stock markets for one hour when the Dow Jones Industrial Average falls 250 points or more within a trading day. The pause is designed to allow time for the markets to absorb the news that precipitated the decline. Should the average fall another 150 points within the same day, trading would again be halted, this time for two hours.

Class A/Class B shares shares of stock issued by the same company but having some difference, such as voting rights, or a dividend preference, or participation. Class B shares are normally the less desirable shares and can also be less expensive.

clearing corporations organizations, such as the National Securities Clearing Corporation (NSCC), that are exchange-affiliated and facilitate the validation, delivery, and settlement of securities transactions.

CLO at the close. By choosing CLO, your order will be executed as near the closing price as possible. Please note that the closing price is not guaranteed as the purchase or selling price.

common stock security representing partial ownership interest in a corporation. Ownership may also be shares of preferred stock, which have prior claim on any dividends to be paid and, in the event of liquidation, to the distribution of the corporation's assets. Common stockholders assume the primary risk if business is poor and realize greater gains in the event of success. They also elect the board of directors that controls the company.

covered call writing an investor who owns stock and sells a call option against the stock giving someone the right to take the stock away from him if the stock value is above the selected strike price upon expiration of the option. If the stock value is below the strike price of the call option, you keep the premium received when selling the call. The writer of the covered call makes a profit or loss on the stock that is called away depending on the purchase price (the cost base).

contract size in futures and options, the size or amount of an asset to be delivered. For example, stock options nearly always specify 100 shares, while a silver futures contract on the Chicago Mercantile Exchange stipulates 5,000 troy ounces.

covering getting out of a short position. When one is short in a stock, one needs to buy back the borrowed shares to close out the trade. This can create either a profit or a loss to the investor depending on the cost of the stock at the time it was shorted.

credit spread the simultaneous sale of one option and purchase of another option that results in a credit to the investor's account. Thus, more funds are received from the sale than are required for the purchase.

current market value the value of an individual's portfolio when the securities are appraised at current market prices. This may vary when using a margin account.

current ratio a company's current assets divided by its current liabilities. Many long-term investors use this ratio to determine the strength of a company.

day trade a trade that is opened and closed the same day.

day trader an investor who buys and sells stock the same day, and win or lose the investor is fully back to cash by the market close of that day.

delayed opening an intentional delay in the opening transaction of a particular security. Generally, the delay occurs when unexpected developments occur before the opening making it difficult for the specialist to match buy and sell orders.

delta the change in the price of an option that results from a one-point change in the price of the underlying stock. For example, a delta of 0.5 indicates that the option will rise in price by $1/2$ point ($.50) for each one-point ($1.00) rise in the price of the underlying stock. Call options have positive deltas; put options have negative deltas.

diagonal spread any spread with different strike prices in which the purchased options have a longer maturity than the written options.

dip a small, short decline in the price of a security.

discount brokerage firm a brokerage firm that discounts commissions for individuals to trade securities. Most discount brokerage firms offer limited advice but reduce their fees by 50 percent or more compared with full-service brokerage firms.

discretionary account written approval by an investor giving the money manager the right to buy/sell securities at his discretion, without prior contact, as long as established parameters are followed.

dividend a share of a company's net proceeds distributed by the company to its stockholders. The amount is decided by the board of directors and is usually paid quarterly.

double witching a term used for the day when both options and futures expire.

Dow Jones Industrial Average (DJIA) a trademark for one of the oldest and most widely quoted measures of stock market price movement. The average is calculated by adding the share prices of 30 large, seasoned industrial firms such as IBM, Exxon, AT&T, and GM and dividing the sum by a figure that is adjusted for such things as stock splits and substitutions.

downgrading a reduction in the quality rating of a security by brokerage firms. Downgrades can affect the value of a stock, creating a drop in the price of the security. Downgrades by certain brokerage firms have different effects on different stocks.

downtick occurs when the bid price drops one level to the next lower price.

downtrend a series of price declines in a security or the general market.

earnings the income of a business. Earnings usually refer to after-tax income but may occasionally be summarized with before-tax revenues. The value of a company's stock can be related to its earnings each quarter of a year. Companies that continue to show strong earnings tend to be more favorable to most investors.

earnings per share (EPS) an earnings measure calculated by subtracting the dividends paid to holders of preferred stock from the net income for a period and dividing that result by the average number of common shares outstanding during that period.

equity in a brokerage account, the market value of securities minus the amount borrowed. Equity is particularly important for margin accounts, for which minimum standards must be met.

ex-dividend date refers to a stock no longer carrying the right to the next dividend payment because the settlement date occurs after the record date. This is the date when a security begins trading without the dividend (cash or stock) included in the contract price.

exercise price the dollar price at which the owner of an option can force the writer to sell an asset (call option) or to buy an asset (put option).

expiration date the last day on which an option holder may exercise an option. This date is stated in the contract at the time the option is written.

fill or kill order an order sent to the floor of an exchange, demanding that an order either be filled immediately and in full or be canceled. It doesn't assure that the order will be entirely filled at the same price. Also known as an **FOK order**.

foreign a non-U.S. company with securities trading on the Nasdaq Stock Market.

full-service brokerage firm a brokerage firm that provides a wide range of services and products to its customers, including research and advice. Its fees may be higher than those of discount brokerage firms.

fundamental analysis (fundamentals) the study of a company's financial reports, marketing, management, and overall business characteristics as a means of determining the value of a stock.

gap opening the opening trade of a security in which the opening price shows a significant increase or decrease compared with that security's closing price of the previous day.

going public a price by which a privately held company sells a portion of its ownership to the general public through a stock offering. Owners generally take their firms public because they need additional large sums of equity funding that they are unable or unwilling to contribute themselves.

good till canceled an order either to buy or to sell a security that remains in effect until it is canceled by the customer or executed by the broker. Also known as an **open order**.

halting of a security a situation where a security is temporarily not available for trading (e.g., market makers are not allowed to display quotes). Halting of a security is common prior to or during market hours when a stock value can be affected by either good or bad news.

in the money used to describe a call (put) option that has a strike price considerably less (more) than the market price of the underlying stock. A deep in-the-money option is also certain to be exercised on or before its expiration.

initial margin requirement the amount of equity a customer must deposit when making a new purchase in a margin account. Margin accounts apply to stocks but are not allowed for the purchase of an option.

initial public offering (IPO) a company's initial public offering, sometimes referred to as "going public," is the first sale of stock by the company to the public. Companies making an IPO are seeking outside equity capital and a public market for their stock.

institutional investor a bank, mutual fund, pension fund, or other corporate entity that trades securities in large volumes.

intrinsic value the amount, if any, by which an option is in the money. This is determined by subtracting the current trading price of the stock from the strike price of the option. The difference in value is known as the intrinsic value or equity.

IRA individual retirement account where contributions are tax deductible and gains are tax deferred.

LEAPS (long term equity anticipation securities) options with an extended expiration date, usually out one and two years, and written in January of those years.

limit an order in which you can set the maximum price you want to pay for your purchase or a minimum price you will accept as seller. Limit orders can be used for both buying/selling of stocks and options.

long-term gain a gain on the sale of a capital asset where the holding period was six months or more and the profit was subject to the long-term capital gains tax.

margin the amount of equity as a percentage of one's current market value in a margin account.

margin account an account in which a brokerage firm lends a client part of the purchase price of securities.

margin call a demand for a client to deposit money or securities when a purchase is made in excess of the value of a margin account, or if the collateral (margin securities) goes down in value.

market maker a dealer willing to accept the risk of holding securities to facilitate trading in a particular security or securities.

market order an immediately executed order to buy or sell a stock or option at the best available price. Your order may get executed at a price different from what you expected. (Be very careful, as market orders are normally not the most desirable prices.)

market value the price at which an investor will buy or sell each share of common stock at a given time.

married put when an investor buys a stock and on the same day buys a put option on the same stock.

Moving Average an average that moves forward with time, dropping earlier components as current components are added. This is an analytical tool that smooths out the fluctuations of a stock chart.

naked option an opening transaction in an option when the underlying asset is not owned. An investor writing a call on 100 shares of IBM without owning the stock is writing a naked option. If the stock is called by the option holder, the writer must purchase shares in the market for delivery and is therefore caught naked.

naked position a security position, either long or short, that is not hedged. For example, an investor short 500 shares of IBM with no other position in IBM stock (i.e., ownership of calls) has a naked position in that security. Because a naked position subjects the investor to large potential gains or losses, it is an aggressive investment position.

New York Stock Exchange the trademarked name of the largest and oldest organized securities exchange in the United States. The NYSE, founded in 1792, currently trades about 85 percent of the nation's listed securities. Most large publicly traded firms' stock, including all those listed in the Dow Jones Averages, list their stock on the NYSE.

news driven any news about a security, or stock, that affects the volatility or the movement of that particular stock.

nondiscretionary account clients must give consent for any purchase or sale before the trade is made, either in person or by phone.

odd lot security trade made for less than the normal trading unit (termed a round lot). In stock trading, any purchase or sale of less than 100 shares is considered an odd lot.

opening the beginning of a trading session. The initial price at which a security trades for the day.

open order an order to buy or sell a security that remains in effect until it is either canceled by the customer or executed.

OPG at the opening. By choosing OPG, your order will be executed at the opening price. If it is not executed at the opening, it will be canceled automatically.

options the right to either buy or sell a specified amount or value at a fixed exercise price. An option that gives the right to buy is a call option. An option that gives the right to sell is a put option. Options expire every third Friday of each month.

Options Clearing Corporation (OCC) an organization, established in 1972, to process and guarantee the transactions in options that take place on the organized exchanges.

option cycle the series of months during which option contracts expire. Options for a particular stock or index generally expire on the same four months every year plus the current and following month.

option premium the sum of money one pays for an option or receives for an option.

out of the money used to describe a call option with a strike price significantly above the market price of the underlying stock. A deep out-of-the-money call or put option is priced significantly lower because in all likelihood it can expire worthless.

over the counter (OTC) a security that is not listed or traded on a major exchange.

order a customer's instructions to buy or sell securities.

paper trade a trade recorded and tracked, but not using actual funds in a brokerage account. Such trades are done as a means of learning and testing strategy.

penny stock a low-priced, speculative stock.

pink sheets the daily sheets that contain the wholesale price quotations for thousands of over-the-counter stocks as listed by dealers who act as market makers in the individual securities.

position investment stake in a security.

position trader a security trader who holds a position overnight and, in some cases, for even longer periods.

premium amount of a bond selling over par, or the cost of an option.

proxy the written authority to act or speak for another party. Proxies are sent to stockholders by corporate management in order to solicit authority to vote the shareholders' shares at the annual meetings.

publicly traded company a company whose shares of common stock are held by the public and are available for purchase by investors.

put option an option contract that gives the owner the right to force the sale of a certain number of shares of stock at a specified price on or before a specific date. Done only in increments of 100 shares (contract).

put spread an investment in which an investor purchases one put on a particular stock and sells another put on the same stock but with a different expiration date, exercise price, or both.

range rider a stock that has highs and lows on its price range and gradually rises to a high range over a period of time.

resistance the upper level of a stock's trading range at which a stock's price appears to be limited in upward movement. Normally indicates that there are more sellers than buyers. Going through resistance is called a "break-out."

reverse stock split an increase in the stock's par value by reducing the number of shares outstanding.

rolling options a strategy when buying calls or puts on a channeling stock. Stock shows a consistent pattern of traveling up and down between two levels, the top being the resistance and the bottom being the Support Level.

rolling out buying back the existing option (closing the position prior to expiration) and rewriting with a different expiration date and strike price. Commonly used when selling naked puts and investors don't want the stock to be put to them.

round trip paying a commission on a buy and a sell trade.

scalper an in-and-out trader who attempts to profit on relatively small price changes. Commonly used by day traders who buy and sell daily for small profits.

short sale the sale of a security that must be borrowed to make delivery. The investor borrows stock from the brokerage house to sell with hopes of repurchasing it at a lower price for a profit. It is done regularly by brokers when a stock can't justify its current high price or when investors believe the market is showing signs of a sell-off.

short-term gain the profit realized from the sale of securities or other capital assets held six months or less.

specialist a member of a securities exchange who is a market maker in one or more securities listed on the exchange. Specialists are assigned securities by the exchange and are expected to maintain a fair and orderly market on them.

spread being a buyer and a seller of the same type of option with the options having different exercise prices and/or expiration dates; the difference between the bid and the ask for a stock or option.

stock an instrument that signifies an ownership position in a corporation.

stock dividend payment of a corporation dividend in the form of stock rather than cash. The stock dividend may be additional shares in the company, or it may be shares in a subsidiary being spun off to shareholders. Stock dividends are often used to conserve cash needed to operate the business. Unlike a cash dividend, stock dividends are not taxed until sold.

stock split the division of outstanding shares of a corporation into a larger or smaller number of shares. For example: In a three-for-one split, each holder of 100 shares before would have 300 shares, although the proportionate equity in the company would remain the same. A reverse split occurs when the company reduces the total number of outstanding shares, but each share is worth more.

stop-loss order sell order placed on a stock below the current market price; if the stock price falls to this price, it automatically becomes an open order sell to at the market to prevent further loss.

stop order an order to buy or to sell a security when the security's price reaches or passes a specified price.

strike price the price at which the underlying security will be bought or sold if the option buyer/seller exercises his or her rights in the contract prior to the option's expiration date.

Support Level the lower point of a stock's chart pattern used as an indication to determine if a stock can return to an upward direction or break below its Support Level and drop in value. Typically it's a price at which there is more demand than supply; stock usually bottoms out due to more buyers than sellers (e.g., a stock sits just above $30 but doesn't go below $30).

suspended trading the temporary suspension of trading in a security. Trading in a security may be suspended if, for instance, a major announcement by the issuing company is expected to influence significantly the security's price. The temporary halt in trading is intended to give the financial community enough time to hear the news. (Also called **trading halt**.)

takeover the acquisition of controlling interest in a firm. Although the term is often used to refer to acquisition by a party hostile to the target's management, many takeovers are friendly.

10-K an annual report of a firm's operations filed with the SEC. Compared with the typical annual report sent to stockholders, a 10-K is much less attractive; however, it contains many more detailed operating and financial statistics, including information on legal proceedings and management compensation. A firm's stockholders may obtain a free copy of the 10-K by writing to the corporate treasurer. (Also called form 10-K.)

thin float small number of shares available for purchase or sale on the market. This can tend to drive the stock value up due to lack of shares, which can create more demand.

tick a movement in the price or price quotation of a security or contract.

ticker symbol a trading symbol used by a company to identify itself on a stock exchange.

time value whatever the premium of the option is in addition to its intrinsic value.

trading halt see **suspended trading**.

trading post Physical location on a stock exchange floor where particular securities are bought and sold. It is here the specialist in a particular security performs his market-making functions and that the crowd (floor brokers with orders in that security) congregates. The New York Stock Exchange, for example, has 22 trading posts, most handling around 100 stocks.

trailing stop a stop order to sell (or buy) a security in which subsequent stop orders are placed at progressively higher (or lower) levels as the stock price increases (or decreases).

trend line in technical analysis, a straight line or two parallel straight lines that indicate the direction in which a security has been moving, and, many chartists believe, the direction in which it will continue to move. When a security price breaks through a trend line, the beginning of a new trend is indicated.

triple bottom in technical analysis, a chart formation of a stock or a market index that has attempted to penetrate a lower price level on three different occasions. If the stock price or index actually breaks through on the downside during the third attempt, it is a bearish signal and the investor should sell or sell short the stock or index. If the stock or index is unable to penetrate the price level, it is a bullish sign that the price is at a strong Support Level.

triple witching hour the hour before market closing when options and futures on stock indexes expire on the same day, thereby setting off frenzied trading in futures, options, and underlying securities. Traders and arbitrageurs unwind investment positions and produce large price movements in securities. The triple witching hour occurs on the third Fridays of March, June, September, and December.

upgrading an increase in the quality rating of a security issue. An upgrade may occur for a variety of reasons, including an improved outlook for a firm's products, increased profitability, or a reduction in the amount of debt the firm has outstanding. As circumstances change, upgrading or downgrading of a security takes place once the issue has been initially rated and sold. An upgrading generally can be expected to have a positive influence on the price of the security.

uptick rule a SEC rule that prohibits the sale of borrowed stock when the last price change in the stock is downward. Part of the Securities Exchange Act of 1934, the uptick rule is designed to keep investors from manipulating stock prices downward by borrowing and selling shares in a declining stock.

volatile in reference to the stock market and to stocks or securities, this is when the market or a particular stock's price tends to vary often and wildly.

volume the amount of trading sustained in a security or in the entire market during a given period. Especially heavy volume may indicate that important news has just been announced or is expected.

index

Technical Indicator Course

Complete home study course covering the most common technical indicators used in today's market. The course gives investors the ability to identify bullish and bearish movements for individual stocks and indexes. The complete course includes 14 video/audio CDs that cover:

- **MACD INDICATOR**
- **MOVING AVERAGES**
- **MONEY STREAM**
- **RELATIVE STRENGTH**
- **REAL TIME EXECUTION**
- **TIME SEGMENTED VOLUME**
- **DISCIPLINE FOR TRADING**

- **STOCHASTICS**
- **STOCK SCANS**
- **VOLUME BARS**
- **BOLLINGER BANDS**
- **BALANCE OF POWER**
- **CORPORATE STRUCTURING**
- **SUPPORT & RESISTANCE LEVELS**

[ ] **YES!** Please send me your Technical Indicator Course. **$289.00**

Monthly CD Club

Being a member of the monthly CD Club is an exciting way to receive information on a regular basis on several different stock market topics such as:

- **STOCK PICKING SCANS**
- **INVESTMENT STRATEGIES**
- **TECHNICAL INDICATORS**
- **INTERVIEWS WITH SUCCESSFUL TRADERS**
- **AND MUCH MORE!**

[ ] **YES!** Please include me in the exciting Monthly CD Club, and bill my credit card monthly. **$14.99/month**

Name:

Title: Company:

Address:

City: State: Zip:

Phone: (   )   Email:

Type of payment:

VISA/MC   Acct. Number: Exp. Date:

To place your order, fax/mail this form to:

Rolling Along Investments, Inc.
5325 Elkhorn Blvd. #320
Sacramento, CA 95842
Phone: (916) 784-2737
FAX: (916) 784-2636